HEINEMANN
Integrated Skills
elementary

MARGARET CALLOW
SERIES EDITOR PHILIP PROWSE

HEINEMANN

Heinemann International
A division of Heinemann Publishers (Oxford) Ltd
Halley Court, Jordan Hill, Oxford OX2 8EJ

OXFORD LONDON EDINBURGH
MADRID ATHENS BOLOGNA PARIS
MELBOURNE SYDNEY AUCKLAND SINGAPORE TOKYO
IBADAN NAIROBI HARARE GABORONE
PORTSMOUTH (NH)

ISBN 0435 28230 1

First published 1990

Acknowledgements

The author would like to thank the following for their help with listening material:
Corinne Duheg, Anna Davies, Paul Callow, Tony Hopwood, Pete Simmons, Nicky Stranks, Pam Gasdby, Judith
Wilson, Philip Prowse, Jane Moates, Joyce Parish, Mike Hughes, Mike Trees.

While every effort has been made to trace the owners of the copyright material in this book, there have been
some cases where the publishers have been unable to find sources or contact the owners. We should be grateful
to hear from anyone who recognises their copyright material and who is
unacknowledged. We shall be pleased to make the necessary corrections in future editions of the book.

**The author and publisher would like to thank the following for their kind permission to use
their material in this book.**
Heinemann Educational Books, for extracts from **The Blue Carbuncle** from **Silver Blaze** by Sir Arthur Conan
Doyle, pp.58 and 59; extract from **The Last Recording** by Tony Hopwood, p.60; Oxford University Press 1981;
Reproduced from the **Oxford Elementary Learner's Dictionary of English** (1981) by permission of Oxford
University Press, pp.13, 39 and 51; Times Educational Supplement
US Prodigy Pulls off Degree Coup, p.12.

Photographs
Barnaby's Picture Library pp.5, 34, 40, 41; Michael Boyd pp.4, 39, 44 (top centre) 46 (top and bottom), 51;
Britain on View (BTA/ETB) pp.22 (top left, top centre, bottom left, bottom right), 44 (top left, top right and
bottom); Great Universal p.15; Sally and Richard Greenhill p.22 (cyclists); Les Sullivan pp.2, 16, 56, 60, 61.

Illustrated by
Nancy Anderson pp.10, 11, 17, 21, 44, 46
Madeleine Baker pp 37, 47
Barbara Crow pp.29, 32, 33, 35, 36
John Gilkes pp 3, 4, 32
Chris Price pp 26, 27, 28
Anthony Sidwell pp.24, 45

Cover by Carrie Craig

Printed in Great Britain by
Thomson Litho Ltd, East Kilbride, Scotland

92 93 94 95 10 9 8 7 6 5 4 3

Contents

Map of the book

	SKILLS	**VOCABULARY**

UNIT 4 A WEEKEND AWAY

LESSON

10	Choosing a Weekend Break	Discussing holidays Reading a letter Reading leaflets Filling in a form	Tourist brochures
11	Choosing Leisure Activities	Listening to plans Reading a postcard Reading an information board Making arrangements and bookings Writing a postcard	Sports
12	Describing Food and Drink	Talking about food Making notes Reading a lunch menu Reading a letter Completing a letter	International dishes English food

UNIT 5 EXHIBITION

13	Describing People	Reading a brochure Making notes Listening to descriptions Writing a description of a person	Descriptions of people
14	Describing Character	Answering a questionnaire Describing characters Reading birth signs Writing a character description	Descriptions of character
15	Pen-friends	Reading advertisements Writing an advertisement Reading a letter Writing a letter	

UNIT 6 FESTIVALS

16	Hallowe'en	Reading newspaper articles Listening to instructions Doing a puzzle Writing a description of an event	Hallowe'en
17	Ghost Stories	Answering a questionnaire Listening to a story Describing feelings Reading a story	Superstitions Feelings Size
18	Traditional Recipes	Listening to instructions Writing a recipe	Recipe Instruction Ingredients Kitchen utensils

		SKILLS	VOCABULARY

Introduction

This book is for elementary to pre-intermediate students and is intended to follow the language of an elementary course. It aims to provide learners with the following:

- a wide range of language through authentic and semi-authentic reading and listening materials
- strategies to handle longer texts in English
- strategies for listening
- vocabulary building skills
- confidence to use unfamiliar material in English
- motivation and interest to produce English in an active way.

The book is made up of ten units. Each unit consists of three lessons. The third lesson in each unit is activity based, involving the learner in larger creative tasks which draw on the language and develop the skills taught in the two preceding lessons. The topics of these activities are:

- class survey
- discussion on language learning
- auction
- discussion on food
- writing to pen-friends
- recipes for festival occasions
- making a class magazine
- designing a tourist brochure
- preparing a radio programme
- writing a mystery story.

The level is graduated so that the later units require more of the learner than the earlier ones, where more skills guidance and help with vocabulary are provided.

It is not necessary to work through all the lessons of a unit. The teacher may decide that a particular lesson fits in with the theme of the coursebook, or may wish to do more intensive practice of certain skills. The map of the book will help the teacher select what is best for the learners.

The skills are integrated in the lessons with, for example, reading helping the listening skill (Auction, Lesson 8) and vice versa (Favourite Holidays, Lesson 23).

In the early lessons oral work is guided through the use of questionnaires. It is intended that pair work and group work be used where possible in the reading and listening tasks to provide more student interaction.

Writing is guided through most of the lessons. The learners are not expected to write something they have not already seen in a reading text. However, they are encouraged to develop their own versions using their own ideas as much as possible.

The tapescript can be used as a learning aid for the learner who lacks confidence in listening.

The vocabulary range is wide. The learner is not expected to understand every word. The aim is for learners to become accustomed to handling a wider range of language and to develop the appropriate techniques to do so. Key vocabulary areas are listed on the contents map. The teacher can select which items of vocabulary the learners need for active use or passive recognition depending on their level. The tasks are designed to help learners decide for themselves how to distinguish between essential and non-essential vocabulary. Guidance is given in the Teacher's Notes on when vocabulary needs to be taught before a particular reading or listening task.

Where appropriate, the material is exploited using tasks which simulate real life situations. Much of the material is authentic. The tasks that go with this material are designed to help the learner understand what is relevant at his/her stage of learning. The rest is semi-authentic in that it is based on 'real' material, but is more accessible to learners of this level.

The Teacher's Notes on p62 give guidance on exploiting the material and some additional suggestions.

1 Describing Your Room

1 Corinne lives and works in Cambridge where she has a flat.

a How many objects in her room can you name?
b Read what Corinne says about her room. Find each object in the photo.
c What does she not talk about?

The patterns in the rug are diagonals and zig-zags which remind me of Crete. That's why I bought it. The colours are very intense.

The spot-light, the blind and the bookcase are all the same colour.

I have a futon which is a kind of sofa bed.

... my desk which is, in fact, my music cupboard.

... my octagonal table which suits the small room. I chose it to be octagonal because I have octagonal plates.

I got this cushion when I was on holiday in Greece.

These are extremely useful wooden boxes. They didn't look very good when I got them and I cleaned them myself.

2 a Guess the colours of these objects in Corinne's room.

futon blind spot lights Greek cushion rug

Choose the colours from the list below.

red brick red blue brown maroon black yellow green

b Listen to what Corinne says and check your answers in **2a**.

3 What parts of the world does Corinne think of when she sees the colours in her rug?

England Japan Italy Crete Peru France Greece

Listen again.

4 A *futon* is not an English word. Do you know which country it comes from?

5 How do you describe these shapes?

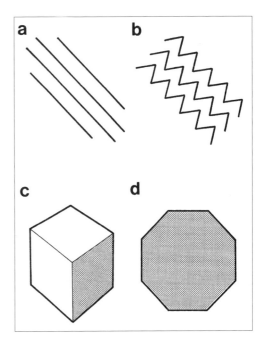

HOMEWORK

Here is a plan of Corinne's room.

Draw a plan of your room.
Label six objects in it.
What colour are they?
Describe each object as Corinne does.

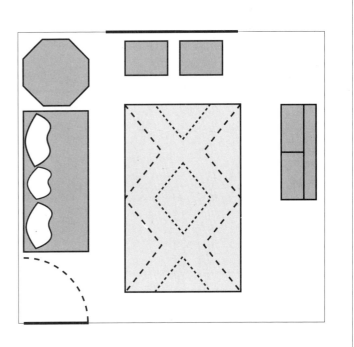

2 Favourite Day

1 Corinne is an archaeologist and works in a museum. Her main interest is bones and skeletons from 200 to 2000 years old.

a Help Corinne label this skeleton using the words below.

hands feet right leg left arm skull neck
back-bone shoulders hips ribs

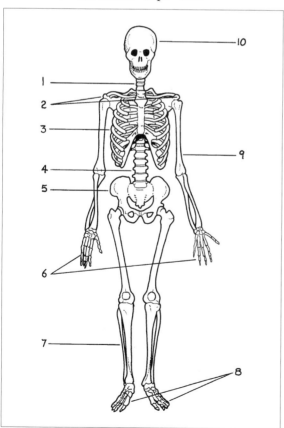

b Read what Corinne says about her favourite day. Does she work on her skeletons?

What's your favourite day?
I think it's Friday. Sunday might be, but it's the day when I know I'm starting back at work on Monday.

What do you do on Friday?
Well, I go into work about 9 o'clock. Usually there's a lot to do because everyone I work with is trying to finish their work by the end of the week.

What do you do for lunch?
I have lunch about 12.30 and most of my friends meet on a Friday lunch-time and we'll have a drink together. In the afternoon, about 3 o'clock the people I work for have gone home. I sort out my work and tidy everything up for the weekend.

What about Friday evening?
When I get home I don't like to go out on a Friday evening. I stay at home and read a book.

2 Complete Corinne's diary for Friday. Choose the answer you think is best from **a**, **b** or **c**.

Remember her main interest is bones and skeletons.

7.30	get up, feed the cat, have breakfast
8.30	cycle to work
9.00	a. put away bones from Thursday
	b. get books from library
	c. talk to friends
11.00	a. get photos of Egyptian mummies
	b. draw map of churches in a 12th century village
	c. find out how much rain there was in 1066
12.30	a. cheese sandwich and an apple for lunch
	b. meet friends for a good lunch and a drink
	c. swimming and yoghurt
3.00	a. go home
	b. continue work on box of 9th century hands
	c. tidy office
evening	a. go to cinema
	b. have friends for meal
	c. read a book

3 Anna is in her last year at school. Listen to what she says about the day she likes best.

  a Which day does she like best?
  b What job does she do?
  c What is the best part of her day?

4 Listen again and complete Anna's diary for the day she likes best.

7.00	get up
8.00–1.00	go to work
	check out the guests
	– – – – – – – – – – –
Lunchtime	get money!
	buy things for evening
	have lunch
2.00–5.00	go back to hotel
	– – – – – – – – – – –
	do school work
	check in new guests
5.00–9.00	go home
	eat dinner
	– – – – – – – – – – –
9.00 till late	get ready to go out
	get bus
	meet friends
	– – – – – – – – – – –

5 Make a diary and fill it in for your favourite day.

6 Look at the interview with Corinne on p 4. Find someone who has the same favourite day as you.

Interview him/her to find out what is the same and what is different.

HOMEWORK

Write the interview you had with your friend. Write your questions and your friend's answers.

3 Describing Personalities

1 Interview four people to find out what entertainment is most popular in your class.

Prepare a poster like this:

TV Singer Song Film Actor Actress Book

You
1
2
3
4

2 Put your results on the class wall chart like the ones below.

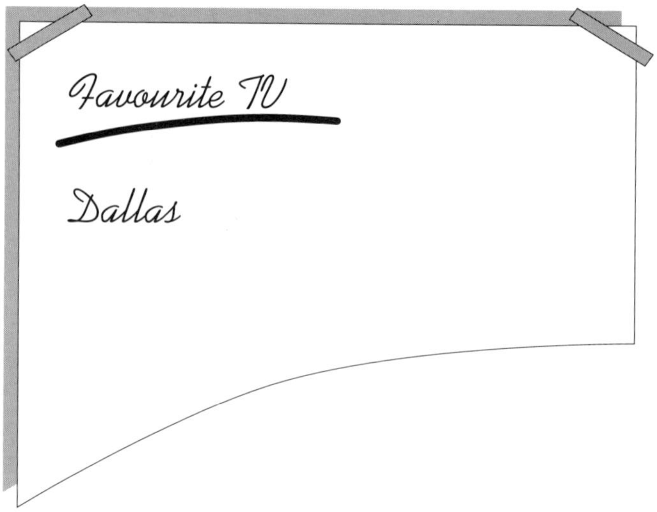

Favourite TV

Dallas

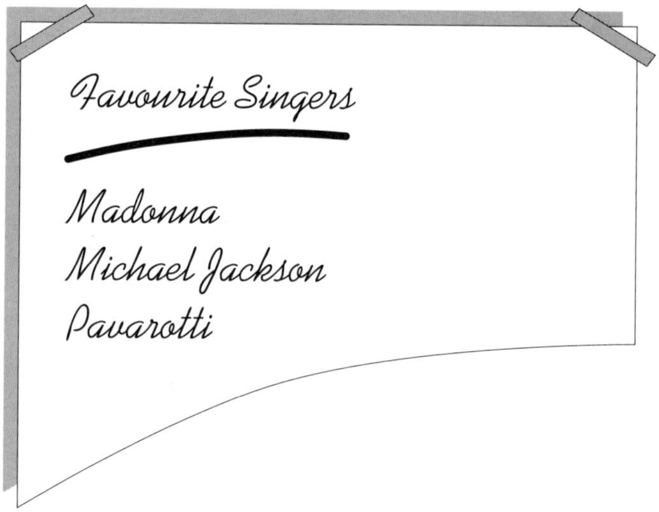

Entertainment Survey

1 What's your favourite TV programme?

2 Who's your favourite singer?

3 What song do you like best?

4 What's your favourite film?

5 Who's your favourite actor/ actress?

6 What book do you like best?

Favourite Singers

Madonna
Michael Jackson
Pavarotti

3 **a** How many of your hobbies are on this list?
cars swimming football reading
listening to music dancing keep fit
making things sport playing a musical
instrument playing cards painting

b Put them in order of importance to you.
c Find someone in the class who has the same interests as you.

4 Find out more about this person. Ask the questions below and make notes.

1 What do you do in your free time?

2 Where do you come from?

3 How long have you been here?

4 What do you do?

5 Do you have any brothers or sisters? Are they older or younger that you?

6 Do you have any pets?

7 What is your birth sign?

8 Have you visited other countries? Which ones?

9 What is your favourite place?

10 Do you have any dreams about what you want to do in life?

11 What makes you happy?

12 What makes you sad?

13 What colour do you like best?

5 Write a profile of your friend. Decide how you want to organise it. The two profiles below will give you ideas.

Description
Nikki is 24 years old and comes from Greece. He is serious.

Likes
He likes Italian food and his favourite singer is Madonna.

Hobbies
He has many hobbies. The most important ones are tennis and swimming. He can also speak more than one language and he likes travelling to different countries.

Family
He has three sisters and lives with his parents.

Work
He studied business and wants to learn English because he needs it for his job.

Rosario
She is 22 years old and lives in Alicante, Spain. She works in a bank and her favourite hobby is computer programming. She doesn't like sports but she does like aerobics. Rosario loves dogs, in fact she has got three dogs. She loves going to the theatre with friends in her free time. She likes the cinema and discos too.
She has been to many countries: France, Germany, Switzerland, Portugal and England. Her great dream is to visit Egypt. She hates getting up early in the morning and loves going to bed late at night.

HOMEWORK

Write your profile so you can compare it with the one your friend is writing.

4 Comparing Study Habits

1 Yuko, Jorge and Isabelle are studying English at a school in England. They talk about how they study after class.

a Make a note of anything that is like the way you study.

b Compare your answers with another person in the class. Are you the same or different?

Yuko from Japan
I'm not a good student. I don't like to do homework. I know it's good for me, but it's boring. So I work with my friends and we talk about it. I find this better. We always do this in the evening. If I work by myself I like lots of loud music and I like sitting on the floor.

Isabelle from Italy
I study a lot. I like to use tapes and the dictionaries in the library in the evening. I stay there for two hours. I write best in the morning before breakfast. No, I don't do any exercise. I like studying, but it is hard work.

Jorge from Spain
I like to study, but I don't like to do it for too long. An hour or two each evening is OK. I like to study in my room because I can work faster, then I like to see my friends and do sports. I work best between 7 and 9 in the evening. I can never work in the morning.

2 Find out more about how you like to study. Try this questionnaire to find out.

3 Compare your answers in **2** with four friends and complete the chart below.

Study Habits

1 When do you like to study?
  a   in the morning
  b   in the afternoon
  c   in the evening
2 How do you like to study?
  a   on your own in silence
  b   on your own with music
  c   with lots of people around
3 When do you think best and write best?
  a   in the morning
  b   in the afternoon
  c   in the evening
4 What do you do before you seriously start work?
  a   tidy your room and put all your papers away
  b   make several cups of coffee
  c   start work immediately
5 Do you find you can do different work at different times of the day?
  a   you can read and make notes at any time
  b   you can write essays best before breakfast
  c   you can think about your reading better in the evening
6 How long do you study at any time?
  a   half an hour then you have a five minutes' break
  b   two hours and then you stop and start again later
  c   fifteen minutes and then you chat to your friends, then another fifteen minutes of study
7 How do you feel before you begin studying?
  a   you look forward to it because you like new ideas
  b   you do it because you have to, but you don't mind
  c   you feel it is something you have to do, but you don't like it
8 How do you feel after you have been studying?
  a   tired but happy
  b   full of ideas and energy
  c   glad it's finished because you don't enjoy it
9 What helps you relax and study better?
  a   sports
  b   yoga
  c   painting or music

WHO LIKES TO STUDY HOW?

NAME				
Early morning Afternoon Evening				
Silence + study Music + study				
Tidy first Lots of coffee Work immediately				
Study 15 mins Study 30 mins Study 2 hours				
Exercise first Exercise after Relax after				
Anything else?				

HOMEWORK

Prepare a study programme for this week using the chart below. Give reasons for your programme.

	Mon	Tues	Wed	Thurs	Fri	Weekend
Early morning						
9.00-3.30			class time			
late afternoon						
evening						

5 Ideas for Vocabulary

1 Professor Black is interested in how people learn. He has some advice for you on how to learn better.

Before you listen to his talk, look at the questionnaire and choose your answers.

1   **a**   Everyone learns in different ways.
    b   There is only one way to learn.

2   **a**   If your work is boring, try again.
    b   If your work is boring, stop.

3   What happens if you study for two hours and have no breaks?

    a   You think clearly at the beginning and end only.
    b   You think clearly all the time.

4   Which is the best way to study?

a

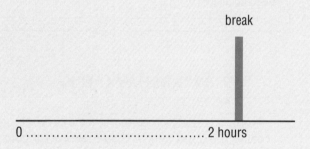

b

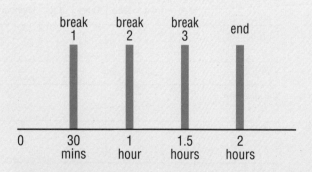

5   **a**   Exercise is bad for the brain.
    b   Exercise helps the brain.

6   **a**   If you want to remember vocabulary, the words must go in the long-term memory.
    b   Short-term memory is best for language learning.

7   When you hear a new word, which ways help you remember it?

    a   Having a picture in your mind.

    b   Having a picture and the word in your mind.

    c   Comparing the English word with a word in your language.

2 Listen to Professor Black's talk and check your answers to **1**.

Do you want to change your study programme in Lesson 4?

3 Take five new words from the last lesson. How do you remember them?

picture in the mind
word and picture
sound and word in your language
putting it into a group
something different

Compare your ideas with a friend.

4 Isabelle and Roula have some problems with vocabulary.

What is wrong? What is your advice?

Isabelle
You know, I like to work in the library. I stay there two hours every evening and I use the dictionary to look up the new words. I write the words in my vocabulary book, then I write the Italian word. It helps to have the Italian, but I don't remember the English word very well.

Roula
I love vocabulary. I write every new word on a little card like this

chat

and I put it on my bedroom wall. I remember the words quite well because I see them every day. I find it difficult to use the words correctly in a sentence. I don't know what's wrong.

H OMEWORK

Begin a vocabulary notebook.

Decide on the best way for you to plan a notebook to help you remember your vocabulary.

Put in five words from today's lesson.

---

8 Which is the best way to note new vocabulary?

a Make a list with translations.

b Organise the words in groups

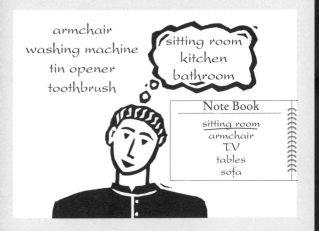

9 Which is the best way to revise new vocabulary?

a Monday   Learn word
  Tuesday   Look again
  Wednesday   Look again
  Weekend   Look again

b Monday   Learn word
  Weekend   Look for second time

6 Reading in a Foreign Language

1 What do you read in your language or in English?

stories magazines newspapers letters

What difficulties do you have reading in English?

2 Isabelle and Jorge find they read in different ways in English.

Who are you like?

Isabelle

I like to understand everything when I read in English. I find newspaper articles very hard, stories are better for me. I read slowly and when I find a word I don't understand, I look it up in my Italian/English dictionary. By the end I understand every word.

Jorge

I don't like to use my dictionary too much and I don't want to spend a long time trying to understand every word. When I have something new to read I look at the title, or headlines if it's a newspaper, to get an idea of the subject. Then I read the article quickly. I understand about 25%, but I have the main idea. Then I read it again more slowly and I understand it more. The third time I read with my dictionary. I think I guess a lot.

3 Read the newspaper article using Jorge's technique. The questions will help you.

 a Look at the title. Can you guess what it will be about?
 b Read the article to check your guess.

THE WORLD'S YOUNGEST GRADUATE

Blue-eyed 11-year-old Californian Adragon Eastwood DeMello has just received a bachelor's degree in mathematics from the University of California at Santa Cruz. He would like to go on to Oxford, Cambridge or London for advanced study in astrophysics or particle physics.

"I want to start learning scientific computer programming next year," he said. "I want to try to understand the creation of the universe."

Adragon has a father who gave up a career as a science writer to educate him. He suspected great things were ahead when his son said "Hello" at the age of six weeks.

Adragon was sent to college at eight because he was always in trouble at elementary school for teaching other children things they were not yet supposed to learn. He finished his two-year course in mathematics and computing in one.

 c How much do you understand?

25%   30%   40%   50%   60%

 d Read the article again more slowly.

Who is it about?
What is he going to do?
Why is he in the paper?

 e Make a note of the words you need to check in your dictionary.

 f Check the words. Use the dictionary opposite to help you.

Dictionary

bachelor *n* **1** man who has never had a wife. **2** person who has the first university degree; *a Bachelor of Arts.*

career *n* job for which special training is needed; *Carol wants a career in sport.*

computer *n* machine that stores information and works out answers.

creation *n* **1** (no *pl*) making something. **2** (*pl* creations) something new that is made; *Mickey Mouse was the creation of Walt Disney.*

degree 1 measure for angles; *There are 90 degrees in a right angle.* **2** measure for temperature; *A person's normal temperature is 37 degrees Centigrade.* **3** title that a university gives to a student who has passed an examination etc; *the degree of M.A.*

4 Did you 'guess a lot', like Jorge?

Which words did you guess?
Were you right or wrong?
Did the guessing help you?

5 Some of the words are blanked out in this paragraph from a detective story. Guess what they are.

I got back to my hotel late. I couldn't ___ . I walked around my room, ___ on the television set, tried to read - but it was no good. My head was ___ of questions. Who was 'Mr Charlie'? What information did Andy Lopez have? I didn't know. I couldn't ___ any more. I was tired now. I was almost ___ . I lay on the bed and closed my ___ .

6 Answer the questions in the Learner Survey.

Compare your answers with a friend.

Learner Survey

1 When you learn a new word, do you learn it better when you:
repeat it in your head?
say it quietly?
write it?

2 When you learn a new word, do you:
want the translation in your language?
want an explantion in English?
want both?

3 When you speak English, if you don't know a word do you:
find other words?
say the word in your language?
use a bi-lingual dictionary?
stop talking?

4 What do you do when you are writing in English and don't know a word?

5 Do you notice when you make mistakes when you speak English?

6 How do you feel when the teacher corrects you?

7 When do you like the teacher to correct you?

8 How do you feel when other students correct you?

9 Do you find it helps your English to make mistakes?

10 How do you feel about speaking and using English:
shy?
strange?
you think everyone is laughing at you?
you are happy to try and see what happens?

HOMEWORK

Start a Learner Diary. After your English lesson, write down:
- what you enjoyed/did not enjoy
- what you found easy/difficult.

7 Describing Clothes

1 Sandra sings in a London pop group. She talks about her clothes.

a How much did she spend?

Hair *The sides are shaved - I do it all myself.*

Jacket *This was £24, I think. I got it from Kensington Market.*

T-shirt with red trim *This T-shirt was about £4, so it wasn't bad value.*

Yellow bag *This is one of my best buys. I got it for £3.99 at Miss Selfridge, and it's really handy.*

Skirt *This is from What She Wants, and it cost me £3.99. I really love that shop because it is so cheap.*

Tights *From Shepherd's Bush Market. I think they were about £1.95 - a bit expensive, but they're really thick.*

Shoes *These were a bit of a bargain. They cost me £18 from a shop down the road from my house.*

b Make a note of the words which show her clothes did not cost very much.

2 What new clothes have you bought in the last two months?

a Make a list of everything you bought.
b Was each item expensive or cheap?
c Interview four people to compare what clothes you bought and prices.

3 Choose something from the catalogue for your birthday.

a Match the description to the picture.
b Decide what you would like and what colour.
c Choose something for two friends in your class.
d Tell your friends what you have chosen.

Fashion Today

a Simple half-sleeve **top** in blue or white. **Pants** in Provencal design, blue on white.

b Checked **shirt** in black, red, blue or green on white.

c **Jacket**, blouse style with striped sleeves in blue or black.

d Black and white **sweater** with diamond pattern.

e Warm casual **jacket** in grey, navy or claret red.

f White cotton **blouse** with flowers. Blue **jeans** with pockets.

g **Shirt**, blue stripes on white.

h Long striped **jacket** in black and white or blue and white.

Top: a simple spotted half-sleeve top with blue or black spots on white.

Skirt: a full skirt in black only.

i Warm **duffle coat** in blue, red or green.

1

2

3

4

5

6

7

8

9

HOMEWORK

1   The auction in Lesson 9 includes clothes.
    Bring in something to sell. Prepare a
    description like that in the catalogue.

2   Describe your favourite weekend clothes.

8 Describing Objects

1 Read this article from the Saffron Walden Weekly News.

GRANGE HALL AUCTION

Grange Hall and its contents will be auctioned next week on July 31st. The last member of the George family, Colonel Arthur George, died last January at the age of 95. The George family has lived at Grange Hall for 200 years and has travelled all over the world.

2 You decide to go to the auction. It begins at 12.00. You arrive at 10.00 so you can see what is for sale.

a Tick (✔) three items in the catalogue that interest you.

GRANGE HALL AUCTION CATALOGUE
16th July 1988

Item　Description

1 An unusual long **knife** with a black wooden handle. The blade is curved and has a flower decoration. Turkish, it was bought in Istanbul in 1917.

2 A **round plate** decorated with two blue and red cocks with red flowers. Greek, about 20 years old.

3 A **wooden antelope**, 6 inches tall. Kenya. About 50 years old.

4 A **map** of an Island in the South Pacific. Colonel George's father bought it to find some lost treasure, but he lost the clues. Dated 1897.

5 An unusual **octagonal plate**, rich brown on cream with some large green and yellow dots. English, late 18th century.

6 A 22 carat **gold ring**. Made in Hong Kong, about 30 years ago.

7 A carved **wooden knife** handle about 4 inches long of a bird eating a man. From the Far East, (Malaysia?), age unknown.

8 A **porcelain vase** with pale blue lines on grey. Modern Japanese

9 A **silver bracelet** decorated with diagonals and small balls. This is Bedouin and comes from the Middle East. It's 50-100 years old.

10 A small rectangular **wooden box**, 6 inches long by 4 inches wide, made of sandalwood. Beautifully carved showing a bird of paradise against a background of leaves. Colonel George's grandfather brought this to England from the Far East.

b Find the items you ticked in the catalogue pictures. Are you still interested?

c Is there anything else that interests you?

3 Listen to the first part of the auction.

   a Make a note of the starting price for each item.

   b Make a note of the finishing price for each item.

4 The words in the catalogue descriptions are mixed up. Put them in the right order.

> **11** a wine small glass red
> **12** a box wooden square
> **13** a silver necklace long
> **14** a Swiss knife small army

5 You go to the auctioneer at the end and ask to buy the Treasure Map for £10. When you get home you find this at the back.

Find the treasure.

Clues

1   *You will not find the treasure in any square of the map where there is a tall coconut tree.*
2   *A large dark cave is a good place for treasure, but you will have no luck.*
3   *Men have died looking for treasure in 3C. They only found large heavy rocks.*
4   *Don't look on any square of the map which shows the long rocky coastline.*
5   *Keep away from anything red or hot.*
6   *The treasure is not in any square which has tall mountains or rocks or round straw huts.*
7   *Water is a clue, but it's not in soft wet ground.*

HOMEWORK

Bring in some objects for the class auction in Lesson 9.

1 Decide which three objects you will sell at the auction.

2 Write a short description of each item for the catalogue.

3 Decide on the starting price you want for each item.

9 Class Auction

In this lesson you are going to have a class auction like the one in Lesson 8.

1 Making the Catalogue

Decide on the name of your auction.

How are you going to arrange your catalogue? Use the one below to help.

GRANGE HALL AUCTION

Item	Description	Starting Price

a Work in groups of four to prepare your catalogue.

b Check the objects for sale in your group and put them in the middle of the table.

c Look at the descriptions you have written for homework for Lesson 7 and Lesson 8. Do you want to make any changes? Your group will have about sixteen items to sell.

d Choose a maximum of eight items for your catalogue.

e Decide on the order you want to sell each item.

f Decide on a starting price (Maximum £10).

g Make the catalogue on a poster. Put each item in the order you want to sell it.

h Put your catalogue on the wall where everyone can see it. Put your items for sale in front of your catalogue.

2 The Auctioneer

a In your group of four, decide who will be the auctioneer (the person who sells the objects) for your group. The rest are buyers.

b The Auctioneer looks at Notes for Auctioneers on p19.

3 Buyers: Pre-auction

a Go round the auction. Look at the items for sale in the other groups. Look at their catalogues and starting prices.

b You have only £20 to spend. Decide what you would like to buy and make notes like the ones below.

c Decide what your highest price will be for each item.

Auction Notes

Group 1

Item		Starting Price
3	Postcard-London	25p
7	Red shirt	£1

Group 2

Item		Starting Price
1	Cassette	£1.50
4	Book	50p

4 The Auction

Procedure

a   Group 1's Auctioneer will begin. All groups listen.

   He/she will describe each item and ask for a price.

b   You can give your price by:
   nodding your head
   putting up your hand
   saying your price, for example, *I give £20.*

c   .Remember you only have £20 to spend. Make a note of what you paid each time you bought something.

5 Notes for Auctioneers

Read your Notes, then have a practice auction with the other auctioneers before the real auction begins.

a   The Auctioneer for Group 1 begins, followed by Group 2 and so on.

b   Stand beside your catalogue. Make sure you know where each item is.

c   Describe each item. Use the catalogue and hold up each item.

d   When Group 1's Auctioneer has finished, Group 2's Auctioneer begins.

Useful language

Opening the auction
Good afternoon ladies and gentlemen. Welcome to this afternoon's auction. We start with items from Group 1.

Describing the objects
Item number 1, if you look in your catalogues, is ...
(Look at the catalogue description.)

Asking for prices
I would like to begin at 50p.
Can I hear ...?
Is that £14 from the gentleman at the back?
Any more ...?

Selling
Going, going, gone. Sold to the lady in red.

Closing the Auction
This is the end of the auction. Thank you, ladies and gentlemen, for coming. I hope you enjoyed your morning/afternoon.

HOMEWORK

Write your learner diary for today. Say what you bought at the auction and how much you paid. What did you learn/practise?

10 Choosing a Weekend Break

1 What do you like to do when you have a long weekend (from Friday to Monday)?

go and stay with friends
spend the weekend going to concerts
have a sports weekend
go to the country or to the coast
visit your family
stay at home and sleep
something else

2 What did you do the last time you had a long weekend?

3 Read this letter which arrived this morning.

Leisure Holidays
Conway St
London WC12

date as postmark

Dear Reader,

Congratulations!

Your lucky number has just won you a holiday for two at one of our prize holiday centres.

TO CLAIM YOUR PRIZE

1 Look at the two marvellous weekends you can have and choose the one you want.
2 Fill in the form enclosed.
3 Give the reason for your choice in no more than 50 words.
4 Return this form to us within 14 days.

Now read about the holidays.

LONDON

There is something for everyone in London; a cosmopolitan atmosphere, history, entertainment and excitement. It's great fun and you can enjoy it in any way you wish.

See some of the richest and most interesting treasures in the world in the national museums and galleries. The Natural History and the Science Museums are very popular with children.

Visit Madame Tussaud's where you will find history, horror and today's most famous people, or see the stars at the Planetarium next door.

Go on a leisurely boat trip on the River Thames for an unusual view of traditional and modern London.

Try London's marvellous shopping facilities from fashion boutiques to antique shops.

London is really alive at night. Theatres, cinemas, concerts and clubs all offer you a night to remember.

ACCOMMODATION

The Crown Hotel
All bedrooms have en suite facilities and colour televisions. Snooker, a solarium and a gym are available for guests' use.

HOLIDAY VILLAGE

There is a Subtropical Paradise in the heart of the
village. It is a giant dome that gives you Caribbean
conditions all the year round. Swimming is boring
when you can try the waves, waterchutes, saunas,
whirlpools, thrilling wild water rapids and
waterfalls which combine to offer you an
experience out of this world.

You'll find every kind of indoor and outdoor
leisure facility you could possibly want. There is an
enormous range of sports from badminton to bowls.
Stay in our beautifully designed villas set in
woodland with a view onto a lake or stream.

Accommodation

All the villas have everything you could want
including an outside patio. The kitchen, lounge
area, bathroom and bedrooms are fully equipped
and have TV, radio and fitted carpets.

4 Tick (✔) what you can do in each place.

	Holiday Village	Crown Hotel
stay in a villa		
watch colour TV		
have a lake outside your bedroom		
play badminton		
go shopping for antiques		
go on a boat trip		
have your own bathroom		
relax in a quiet place		
stay in a hotel		
see famous 'people'		
go swimming		

5 Match the words from the brochures in **A** with
the definitions in **B**.

A	B
popular	very large
leisurely	old object
marvellous	carpet from wall to wall
antique	bathroom next to the bedroom
en suite facilities	kitchen which has everything
giant	everyone likes it
dome	very good
fully equipped	a round shape
fitted	relaxing

6 Which holiday do you want?

a Find a friend who wants to go to the same
place.

b Decide how you will spend your time.

HOMEWORK

**Here is the form that came with the letter.
Fill it in to claim your holiday.**

Name:

Address:

Tel. no.

I would like to go to ____ for my weekend.

I like it because ____ .

I want to go from Friday ____

to Monday ____ (include dates).

11 Choosing Leisure Activities

1 What is your favourite sport when you go on holiday?

2 Different people talk about their favourite sports. Match what they say with the photographs below.

I could watch tennis all day long.
I really love swimming.
Canoeing down a river.
Wind-surfing, every time.
Oh, hill-walking, nothing better.
Sailing - out at sea.
I'm learning to ride, so for me horse-riding.
Cycling, it's a family activity.

A

B

C

D

E

F

G

H

3 Nicky is going on holiday next week. She talks about where she is going and why. Listen to what she says and tick (✔) the correct answers.

  a Where is Nicky going to stay?
      In a London hotel.
      In a holiday village.
      In a village by the sea.

  b Why did she choose it?
      It was recommended.
      The weather is good.
      There is a lot to do for small children.
      It is very cheap.

  c How old is Joanna?
      18 years old.
      18 months.
      8 years old.

  d Which activities does Nicky talk about?
      swimming
      football
      tennis
      badminton
      hiring bicycles
      jacuzzis
      dancing

  e Which activity does she want to try?

4 Read Nicky's postcard to find out what she, Joanna and Jeff did.

August 11th
Having a lovely time here. Joanna really loves the swimming pool. I prefer lying under the tropical trees with a drink. Jeff went wind-surfing and really enjoyed it.
This doesn't feel like England!

Love
Nicky

Mr & Mrs D Brown
Rose Cottage
Green Lane
Linton
Cambs

5 You decide to go to Sherwood Forest Holiday Village with three friends. It is a warm weekend in summer.

What are you going to do?
When are you going to do these activities?

Fill in your Activity Plan. Decide how to organise your day there.

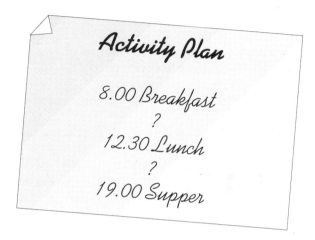

Activity Plan

8.00 Breakfast
?
12.30 Lunch
?
19.00 Supper

Look at the Information Board for ideas.

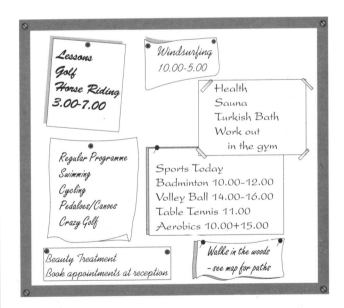

Lessons
Golf
Horse Riding
3.00–7.00

Windsurfing
10.00–5.00

Health
Sauna
Turkish Bath
Work out
  in the gym

Regular Programme
Swimming
Cycling
Pedaloes/Canoes
Crazy Golf

Sports Today
Badminton 10.00–12.00
Volley Ball 14.00–16.00
Table Tennis 11.00
Aerobics 10.00+15.00

Beauty Treatment
Book appointments at reception

Walks in the woods
– see map for paths

HOMEWORK

Write a postcard to a friend about what you did during your weekend.

12 Describing Food and Drink

1 What do you know about food and drink from around the world? How quickly can you do this competition?

   a Which countries do these dishes come from? You may be able to think of more than one country.

   hamburgers   spaghetti bolognaise   curry
   paella   crepes Suzettes   cheese fondue
   fish and chips   chili con carne
   sweet and sour pork   pizza   sate   moussaka

   b Which country is famous for these drinks?

   coke   green tea   warm beer   sake   port
   cognac   tea with milk   whisky   champagne
   vodka   sherry

   c Which food is typically English? Give examples of other English food.

2 Look at the board outside an English restaurant.

TODAY'S MENU

HOMEMADE SOUP

*   *   *

STEAK AND KIDNEY PIE
PLAICE AND CHIPS
SHEPHERD'S PIE
ROAST BEEF AND YORKSHIRE PUDDING
ROAST LAMB AND MINT SAUCE

*   *   *

SALADS
CHEESE, HAM, CHICKEN

*   *   *

VARIETY OF SANDWICHES
DESSERTS - BEER WINES
COFFEE SOFT DRINKS

a Choose what you would like to have for lunch from the board.

b Prepare a similar board for a restaurant which shows typical food from your country.

3 What do the English have for breakfast, lunch and supper?

Write down three things that you think are typical.

4 Jane writes a letter to her American pen-friend about English meals.

Make a note of anything you didn't know.

> Dear Sharon
> Do you really think we have bacon and eggs for breakfast? Most English people have cereal and toast with tea or coffee.
>
> I usually have a small lunch – a sandwich and soup, though a lot of people go to a pub and have pie and chips.
>
> I have my main meal in the evening. I like spaghetti bolognaise or goulash and, if I have time, a good curry.
>
> How about you?
>
> Love Jane

5 What do you eat in your country for breakfast, lunch and supper?

HOMEWORK

Write a letter to Jane telling her about meals in your country.

Use the letter below to help you.

> Dear Jane
> I thought you would like to know what we have for our meals.
> For breakfast we have . . . . . .
> . . . .
> Lunch is a big/small meal. I have
> . . . .
>
> In the evening we have . . . . . .
> . . . .
>
> Yours sincerely

13 Describing People

1 Read the information about a famous English tourist sight.

a Where is it?
b How old is it?
c What can you see there?
d Who goes there?
e How many people go there?

Places to Visit

You can visit one of the most famous collections of waxworks in the world in London. It was begun nearly 200 years ago and today you can see life-like figures of famous people in the past and present.

It attracts the young, the old and people of every nationality. In all, over two million visitors go there every year.

2 Different visitors talk about Alfred Hitchcock, the director of horror films, and David Bowie, the pop singer.

Which comments are about which person?

a *Wow, he looks glamorous.*
b *I always thought he was big, but he looks very solid with those broad shoulders.*
c *That light suit really goes with his fair hair.*
d *Look, there's Hitchcock over there with the small boy.*
e *I'd love thick shiny hair like that.*
f *Um, looks really impressive, those dark brown eyes and that dark suit. Frightens me a bit.*
g *And that neck-tie is the exact blue of his eyes.*
h *He looks really tall on that pedestal, but really he's only medium-height.*
i *He's really short, isn't he?*
j *Really casual the way he's standing there, with his hands in his pockets.*

3 What do they notice about Hitchcock and Bowie?

Make notes about their height, hair, eyes, and clothes.

4 Pam and Judith visit the exhibition. They see the waxworks below.

a Match the waxwork with these famous names.

Agatha Christie   Telly Savalas
Boy George   Liza Minelli   Picasso   JR

b Make a note of three things you think they'll say about each waxwork.

 c Listen to Pam and Judith. Which waxwork do they see first, second, etc? Who are the waxworks? Check your guesses.

 d Listen again. What do they say about each waxwork? Add one more item to your list.

HOMEWORK

Choose someone from your class and write a short description of him/her. Do not write the name. The class will try to guess who it is.

14 Describing Character

1 Judith and Pam describe two of the waxworks

Who are they describing? Look at Lesson 13, p27.

Judith   *He looks a bit of a menacing character, doesn't he?*
Pam   *Yes, a bit frightening.*
Judith   *Looks very respectable.*
Pam   *Doesn't she? Doesn't she look sweet?*

2 How do people see you? Ask a friend to complete this questionnaire about you.

3 Compare your answers.

4 Match these adjectives to each sentence in the questionnaire.

hard-working kind shy honest friendly serious clever happy amusing

5 Find opposites from the list below

easy-going cheerful kind angry unfriendly self-confident dishonest stupid boring

6 Describe these famous people.

WHAT SORT OF PERSON IS HE/SHE?

1   *He/she likes meeting and talking to people.*

2   *He/she says what he/she thinks is right.*

3   *He/she thinks work is more important than leisure.*

4   *He/she enjoys laughing and joking.*

5   *He/she is good at mathematical problems and has a good memory for facts.*

6   *He/she helps other people.*

7   *He/she thinks alot.*

8   *He/she is not very happy when meeting new people.*

9   *He/she makes people laugh.*

7 Compare your descriptions with their birth signs below. Charlie Chaplin is Aries and Joan Collins is Gemini.

Look at your birth sign. Do you agree with it?

ARIES
21st March - 20th April
+ is self-confident, romantic, sporty
- doesn't think about others

TAURUS
21st April - 20th May
+ is calm, patient, musical
- is lazy, boring, gets angry easily

GEMINI
21st May - 20th June
+ is good at language and writing, busy, amusing
- is unable to relax, dishonest

CANCER
21st June-20th July
+ is kind, is good at knowing how other people feel, has a good imagination
- is bad-tempered, has no sense of humour

LEO
21st July-21st August
+ is self-confident, romantic, has a good sense of humour
- is childish, gets angry easily

VIRGO
22nd August-22nd September
+ is hard-working, honest, practical
- has no sense of humour, worries about everything

LIBRA
23rd September-22nd October
+ is easy-going, romantic, thoughtful, polite
- is unable to make decisions, cold, eats too much

SCORPIO
23rd October-22nd November
+ is powerful, has a good imagination, understands other people's feelings
- wants power too much, says what he/she thinks

SAGITTARIUS
23rd November-20th December
+ laughs a lot, is honest, open-minded
- hates detail, is childish

CAPRICORN
21st December-19th January
+ is careful, has a good sense of humour, is kind
- is cold, is not open-minded

AQUARIUS
20th January-19th February
+ is friendly, wants to change things, is very modern
- cares too much about himself/herself, is impatient

PISCES
20th February-19th March
+ is kind, is good at knowing how other people feel, is romantic, musical
- is not good at every day living, is shy, is dishonest

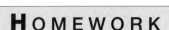

HOMEWORK

Write two short character descriptions.

1   Write a description of yourself.

2   Write a description of someone in the class.

15 Pen-friends

1 You are looking for a pen-friend in a magazine
BBC English. Who do you choose?

I am a 20 year-old engineering student and would like to find pen friends from all over the world. My hobbies are reading, travelling and listening to music.
Roger Jones, Green Trees, Castle Hill, Stamford, Britain.

I am 28 years old and study English at the British Council. I would like to write to anyone interested in travel, cinema and drama.
Marie Haumont, Paris, France.

I'm a 19 year-old University student. I would like to make contact with students abroad. My interests are sport, literature and politics.
Sirio Tripaldi, Milano, Italy.

I would like to find friends worldwide. I am 22 years old and enjoy acting, poetry and photography.
Jennette Costa, Salta, Argentina.

I would like to make friends mainly in Europe. My hobbies are stamp collecting, swimming and travel.
John Gooding, California, USA.

I would like to write English to students anywhere. My hobbies are cinema, cycling and music.
Francis Yaw, Karonga, Malawi.

I'm finishing secondary school this year and want to practise my English. My hobbies are fashion, music, painting and playing the guitar.
Renate Jonker, The Haag, Holland.

I want to write to anyone interested in football, pop music and science fiction stories.
Serpil Arcasoy, Ankara, Turkey.

I am looking for friends everywhere. I am interested in drama, swimming and tennis.
May Mingjian, Beijing PR, China.

2 Write a similar advertisement for yourself.
Include your age and your hobbies or
interests.

3 Beatrix in Belgium saw the same page. Who did she write to?

11 Avenue des Ombrages
Gent
Belgique

Dear ——,

I saw your advertisement for pen-friends. I live in Belgium and would like to meet English people. My hobbies are the same as yours - reading, travelling and I love jazz. I am eighteen years old. I began English six years ago, but I have never been to England. I have always liked my English classes. I am going to study dance and drama next year at college and this year I am working for a local newspaper. It's quite interesting and I can earn some money. In the summer I will stop work for three months so I can travel across India.

Well, that's me! Looking forward to hearing from you.

Best wishes,
Beatrix

4 Write a letter to your new pen-friend. Tell him/her about yourself. Use the outline below to help you.

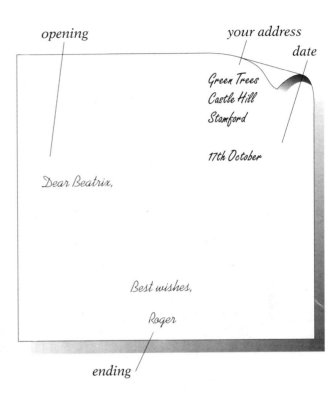

opening   *your address*
                                   date

Green Trees
Castle Hill
Stamford

17th October

Dear Beatrix,

Best wishes,

Roger

ending

16 Hallowe'en

Hallowe'en (Holy Evening) is the night of October 31st, the evening of All Saints Day (November 1st). In the past people believed that on the night of Hallowe'en the dead would rise from their graves to revisit their homes.

The people lit fires to frighten away evil spirits and help the ghosts find their way home. Today people in Britain do not believe this, but some of the customs remain.

1 Look at the picture.

a Who are the people?
b What are they doing?

2 Match the headlines and the articles.

GHOSTS FRIGHTEN OLD LADY

TRICK OR TREAT?

Hallowe'en in Cambridge Tonight

Tonight children all over the town will put on clothes to look like witches or ghosts and visit their neighbours for 'Trick or Treat'.

Last year when the children played 'Trick or Treat' at Hallowe'en most people gave them treats such as apples, nuts, chocolates or sweets. Mr Brown of Perne Avenue said 'no' and closed the door. In the morning he found his roses were not on the rose bush, but all over his car. He doesn't want another trick this year.

'I thought I was dead' says Mrs Smith, aged 90, of Victoria Rd. At eight o'clock last night she heard her door-bell. When she went to the door she saw two white ghosts with plastic bags in their hands. Then one began to talk ...

3 a What treats do the children get?

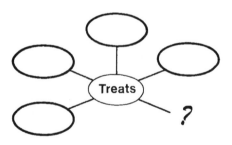

Read the articles again.
b Suggest a treat.
c What trick happened to Mr Brown?
d Suggest two more tricks.

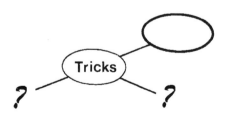

e Why do you think the 'ghosts' were carryng plastic bags?

4 A pumpkin, a large yellow vegetable, is used at Hallowe'en. The inside is taken out and a face is made on the outside.

a Copy the pumpkin and decide what kind of face you would like.

b Label it using words from the list below the pumpkin.

mouth: smiling/sad/funny
eyes: big/small/square/round
nose: long/short/fat/thin

5 How do you make a Hallowe'en pumpkin? Put these sentences in the correct order.

a You put a candle in the pumpkin.
b You cut holes in the pumpkin.
c You buy a pumpkin.
d You make eyes, a nose and a funny mouth.
e You put the lid on.
f You put the pumpkin in a window.
g You take out the inside.

John's children make pumpkins at Hallowe'en. Listen to his description. Is your order the same?

6 Look at the picture of the children on p32 again. What are the children wearing? Why?

7 Listen to John describing how his children play 'Trick or Treat'.

a What do the children do before they leave the house?

b What happens when they go out?

8 How many Hallowe'en words can you find? The words go down, across, and diagonally.

a	p	f	a	c	e	x
p	u	t	r	i	c	k
p	m	r	n	e	g	g
l	p	e	o	u	h	h
e	k	a	s	e	t	o
w	i	t	c	h	e	s
o	n	s	w	e	e	t

HOMEWORK

Anne wrote in her diary what she did for Hallowe'en. Complete it for her.

MONDAY 31ST OCTOBER

Bob, Eric and Lucy came
to my house at 6.30 and
we began to get ready for
Hallowe'en

17 Ghost Stories

1 How superstitious are you?
Do this quiz and find out.

How superstitious are you?

1 Do you believe in ghosts?

2 Would you walk through a cemetery on your own at midnight?

3 You see a ladder against a wall. Do you walk under it?

4 You hear a strange noise in your house in the middle of the night. Do you go and see what it is?

5 You see a strange light in the sky. Do you think it is a UFO (Unidentified Flying Object) from another planet?

6 Do you believe Uri Geller can bend metal spoons with his mind?

7 A black cat walks in front of you, is this good?

8 Do you believe it is possible to talk to dead people?

If you answered yes to three or more then you are superstitious. Take care on 31st October! If your answers were mainly no then you are very practical. But you may get a surprise at Hallowe'en!

2 Late on Hallowe'en evening, people tell ghost stories.

This is what happened to Fay Merryweather, a stewardess on a plane.

Listen to her story.

Are these sentences true (T) or (F)?

		T	F
a	Flight 318 was flying from New York to Florida.		
b	Fay saw a man's face in the oven door.		
c	She was very frightened.		
d	She ran for help.		
e	The pilot went to the galley with her.		
f	He recognised the face.		
g	Don Repo had died in an air crash twelve months before.		
h	The ghost wrote a message about a fire.		
i	The engine caught fire before the plane landed in Florida.		
j	No one was killed.		

3 This bird appears in a ghost story.

a Label the parts of the bird.

wings   beak   tail   head   claws

b If you saw a bird like this, how would you feel?

bored   interested   frightened
very frightened   terrified

c Put these words in order of size.

large   enormous   tiny   gigantic   little

4 Read the story to find out what the bird does.

THE BIRD

In 1914 there was a story that an office in London was haunted. Two newspaper men decided to see if this was true. So, late one evening, after everyone had gone home they went to the office. They went inside, lit the gas lights (this was before electricity) and locked the door so no one could get in. They also locked the windows. Then they covered the floor with white chalk so they could see if anyone or anything went across it. Nothing happened. By midnight they were beginning to get bored and a bit sleepy. Still nothing. Then suddenly the locked door opened. At the same time the locked windows blew open and a strong wind rushed into the room putting out the gas lights. The two men heard a terrifying noise, like the beating of gigantic wings and in the moonlight they saw a large shape go across the room and disappear through the wall. The lights came on again by themselves. The two men looked at each other, then at the windows and the door. Everything was locked. But in the chalk on the floor they saw the prints of enormous claws like those of a giant bird. The frightened men ran from the room and never went back.

HOMEWORK

1 Answer the questions.

a What did the men do before midnight?
b How did they feel at midnight?
c What happened to the doors, windows and lights just after midnight?
d What did the men hear?
e What did the men see?
f Then what happened to the doors, windows and lights?
g What did the men see on the floor?
h What did they do?

2 Find words in the story which match the definitions below.

a had a ghost in it
b closed with a key
c not interested
d came quickly
e very frightening
f a regular sound

18 Traditional Recipes

1 Here is some information about another British custom; the Pancake Race on Pancake Day.

   a Look at the picture and the descriptions. Which is the best description of the picture?

(i) Pancakes: flat sweet cakes made from eggs, butter, sugar, flour and milk.
(ii) Pancake Day
(iii) The Tuesday before Lent begins, 40 days before Easter.
(iv) A race. Everyone has a pancake in a frying pan. They run and toss their pancake. The winner does not drop it.

   b Do you have a custom like this?

2 Look at the pictures for a pancake recipe.
What order do you think they should be in?

a Cook over a high heat.

b Stir the flour and salt in a bowl.

c Put some butter in the frying pan.

d Toss it!

e Put some mixture in the frying pan.

f Make a hole in the middle of the mixture.

g Mix with a whisk.

h Put the pancake in the oven.

i Add the milk slowly and stir.

3 Call-A-Recipe is a telephone service. You dial a number and get a different recipe every day. Listen to Call-A-Recipe to check your answer to **2**.

4 Write a recipe for a well-known dish from your country.

a Work in groups.
b Decide on a recipe.
c Work out the steps needed to prepare it.
d Write it on a poster.

HOMEWORK

1 Write the recipe for pancakes in full for a friend. Use these words:
first   then   next   finally

2 Make some for your supper.

19 Preparing a Health Questionnaire

1 How healthy are you? Try this quiz to find out.

HEALTH QUIZ

1 How many meals do you eat a day?
a three **b** two **c** one

2 What is your first meal?
a breakfast **b** lunch **c** a snack at 11 o'clock.

3 Do you eat snacks between meals?
a never **b** sometimes **c** all the time

4 How often do you eat meat?
a less than four times a week **b** once a day **c** twice a day

5 What do you drink most?
a water **b** coffee **c** fizzy drinks

6 How often do you eat cakes and chocolates?
a three or four times a week **b** once a day **c** several times a day

7 How often do you eat fruit, vegetables and salads?
a three or four times a day **b** once a day **c** three or four times a week

8 How much fried food do you eat each week?
a maybe once a week **b** three or four times a week **c** every day

Score: Give yourself:

2 points for every **a**
1 point for every **b**
0 point for every **c**

12-16 you have a healthy diet
6-12 you need to take care
0-6 time to re-think your diet

2 Look at this daily menu for many thirteen year-olds in Britain.

a What changes would you suggest?

MENU

Breakfast
Milk drink and biscuit plus ice pop on way to school

Morning break
Packet of crisps

Lunch
Chips, milk, packet of crisps, packet of biscuits

Tea
Sausage, egg, bacon, ice lolly
Packet of mints
Fizzy orange drink

b What did you eat yesterday? Write a menu like the one in **2**.
c How healthy is your diet? What changes can you make?

3 Esmé Taylor is a TV Keep-Fit Queen.

a What was Esmé like four years ago?
b What bad habits did she have?
c What does she eat now?
d What happened six months after she began her new diet?
e Give an example of *high calorie food* and *low calorie food* Esmé ate.

Esme Taylor -

Keep-Fit Queen

She smoked, ate snacks, loved cakes, chocolates and cola, but she didn't have much time for a big meal. She is a professional dancer/keep-fit teacher who danced for at least three hours a day, so you can't say she didn't exercise.

'Four years ago I was fat and overweight. I talked to a lot of people about the food I was eating and decided my diet was rubbish. I changed my whole attitude to eating and in six months I was down from a size 14 in clothes to a size 10.
I learnt a lot about the fat in the food we eat and the antibiotics in meat. I stopped eating meat, cakes, chocolates, all sorts of things.
I eat brown bread, fish and lots of vegetables and salads - I feel so much better with this low-calorie diet.'

4 The people of Vilcabamba in Ecuador have a different attitude to a healthy diet.

a What is the average age of the inhabitants of Vilcabamba?
b What is good about their diet?
c What is 'bad'?
d Why do they think they live so long?
e What do you think?

How to live to be 142

The inhabitants of Vilcabamba in Ecuador think it's normal to live to be 100 years old. The possible reason for their long lives is their low-calorie diet. They average 1,700 calories a day, which is half the average in Britain. They eat very little meat - only one ounce per week. Another possible reason for their great age is they drink 2-4 cups of rum and smoke between 40 and 60 cigarettes a day. The valley where they live is quiet and peaceful and the climate mild, which may also explain why they live so long. The Vilcabambans themselves think it is because of the herbal teas they drink.

Dictionary

herb *n.* plant or flower used in medicine or cooking *-al adj*
ounce *n.* approximately 28 grams
rum *n.* alcoholic drink made from sugar

H O M E W O R K

Do a survey of your friends' eating and exercise habits. You will use the information you collect for an article for the Class Magazine in Lesson 21.
a Prepare ten questions. Look at the Health Quiz for ideas.
b Interview at least four people.

20 Reading Factual Information

LONDON MARATHON 1988

WHAT'S ALL THIS MARATHON BUSINESS?

- Of the 22,469 folk who entered, a mighty impressive 21,000 finished.
- The men's winner was Henryk Jorgensen from Denmark, who finished in two hours, 10 minutes and 20 seconds. Ingrid Kristiansen won the women's event in two hours, 25 minutes and 41 seconds.
- Thousands of people dressed up for the race. Amongst this year's fancy dress entrants were a ballerina, a house, an elephant and one misguided soul with a cake on his head.
- Nearly £9 million will be raked in this year through charity competitors and over £1 million of this will go to Great Ormond Street Children's Hospital.
- The oldest runners were Richard Dolfe, who's 82 and 76-year-old granny Jenny Wood Allan, who both finished the race.
- One competitor played his flute continuously during the 26 miles, and was even given requests on his way round the course.
- The London Marathon is regarded as the biggest in the world. Only the New York one can come near the quantity of runners.
- Cheats aren't too common at the Marathon, although some competitors have been caught hopping on trains or thumbing car rides to save themselves a few miles.
- 10 per cent of the entrants were women.
- Some competitors were still running at 6.30 pm - nine hours after the race started.

David Green, 19, is a shop assistant from Barking. He completed the marathon in four hours, seven minutes and says he entered *"to prove I could do it. But once is enough. I've proved my point. It wasn't easy and I broke down in tears at 22 miles but the other runners egged me on. I've had a really great day."*

Marie Williams, 74, says, *"It's a wonderful day, it gives me a great boost. I come down to the park every year to watch the start and it gets better and better."*

James Newman is 18 and Kevin Buckley is 17. They've come to watch Kevin's brother. *"We're not fit enough to enter the race ourselves,"* says Kevin, *"but my brother's good. He'll go the distance, no problem."* Meanwhile, James confesses: *"I drink too much, I eat too much and I do no exercise. I'm a physical wreck."*

---

1 Basic Facts

a How many finished the race?
b How many did not finish it?
c What time did the race begin?
d How long is the race? (1 mile = 1.6 km)
e How much money will the race make?
f Where does the money go?
g What fancy dress did some runners wear?

2 People Facts

a What was the nationality of the winner?
b What was the fastest women's time?
c What was the difference between the fastest woman and the fastest man?
d What was the age of the oldest competitor?
e How long did David Green take?
f What happened to him at 22 miles?
g Who loves watching the race every year?

3 Here is an interview with Mike Johnson, an American pop star. Follow the Editor's instructions.

STOP PRESS   URGENT CORRECTIONS ON THIS INTERVIEW BEFORE PRINTING!!!   Editor

Who's your best friend?
I think dancing is the most wonderful thing of all time. When I dance I feel, I mean, I really feel it and I feel free and I do what I feel.

How much money do you earn?
Well, I suppose you might think it strange to sleep in an oxygen tent, and I bathe in fizzy mineral water every morning.

Where do you come from?
Yes, I'm very fond of children.

Do you like dancing?
From outer space. Really I'm an alien.

Do you like children?
I'm not sure. More than £20 million a year. I give a lot to charity.

Do you have any strange habits?
Cuddles. He's a chimpanzee, but he's a real friend.

4 How many words can you find from the magazine?

CROSSWORD

Across

1 Something to eat between meals. (5)
6 Mike Johnson feels this about children. (4)
7 Past form of eat. (3)
8 You need lots of this to run a race. (6)

Down

2 Chocolate is full of these. (8)
3 To be well. (7)
4 Henryk Jorgensen was the fastest ___ in 1988. (6)
5 Aliens like ET come from there. (5)
9 The waiter gives you one when you go to a restaurant. (4)

H OMEWORK

Interview someone in the class about their interests, for the Class Magazine in Lesson 21.

Use the interview with Mike Johnson for ideas. Use the same layout.

21 Making a Magazine

In this lesson you are going to prepare a class magazine. Your Editor has been given these instructions.

ENGLISH AROUND THE WORLD
MEMO

To: Magazine Team

From: International Editor

1 Decide what news to put in the magazine. You can choose from the Magazine Ideas (attached).
2 Decide who will write each news section. Maximum team size - four.
3 Each mini-team of four people will decide how many items of news to include in each section.
4 When each mini-team has written their section, they must
  a check their spelling
  b decide how to display it on the classroom wall
5 Remember - there isn't much time. Check with your Editor for the dead-line when everything must be finished.

Good luck!

MAGAZINE IDEAS

Class News

Has anyone in the class done anything special like being in the local newspaper, playing for the town football team, going anywhere interesting, doing anything unusual?

Interview this person.

School Diary

Prepare a diary of what will happen in your school next week.

e.g. Monday - Pop quiz evening, bring your favourite records. 19.30

Puzzles/ Crosswords

Do you want to try a crossword in English?

- Decide what words you want to use.

- Write some definitions (look at definitions for the Crossword, Lesson 20 p41).

- Make them into a puzzle shape.

Eating and Exercise Survey

Prepare two typical menus for your class. Find one that is the healthiest and one that has the most unhealthy food. You could use the information collected in Lesson 19, Homework p39.

STORIES

Do you know any strange stories like *How to Live to 142* or any ghost stories like the ones in Lesson 17 p35? Write the story or make up a new story.

Songs/Poems

Do you know any poems in English or the words of any pop songs?

Write what you can remember or make something.

INTERVIEW

Choose anyone in the class to interview. Use the interview with Mike Johnson in Lesson 20 p41 to help you.
Try some of the same questions and add some new questions.

Food Tips

Got any good ideas for eating?
Look the recipe for Pancakes, Lesson 18 p37 for ideas. Interview people in your class for some more ideas.
How many bright ideas can you find?
How about a competition for the best idea?

22 Reading Holiday Brochures

1 These are some of the most popular holidays in Britain.
Match the holidays with the photographs.

1 Walking on the west coast of Scotland.
2 Camping in North Wales.
3 Climbing in the Lake District.
4 The beaches of Cornwall.
5 On a barge on the Norfolk canals.
6 Theatre visits in London.

2 a Copy the map of Britain.

b Write on the map what people like to do in each place.

3 Look at the brochure of North Wales on the opposite page. Where would you find the following?

a the Welsh Mountain Zoo
b the smallest house in Wales
c unusual birds
d an Italian-looking village
e activity holidays
f a beautiful beach

4 Find adjectives from the brochure to describe these places.

a the **biggest** mountain
b a **very good** place for activity holidays
c **well-known**
d a **dream** village
e a **very small** railway
f **very good** views
g **strange** bridges

5 If you were to go to North Wales what three places would you like to see? Give your reasons.

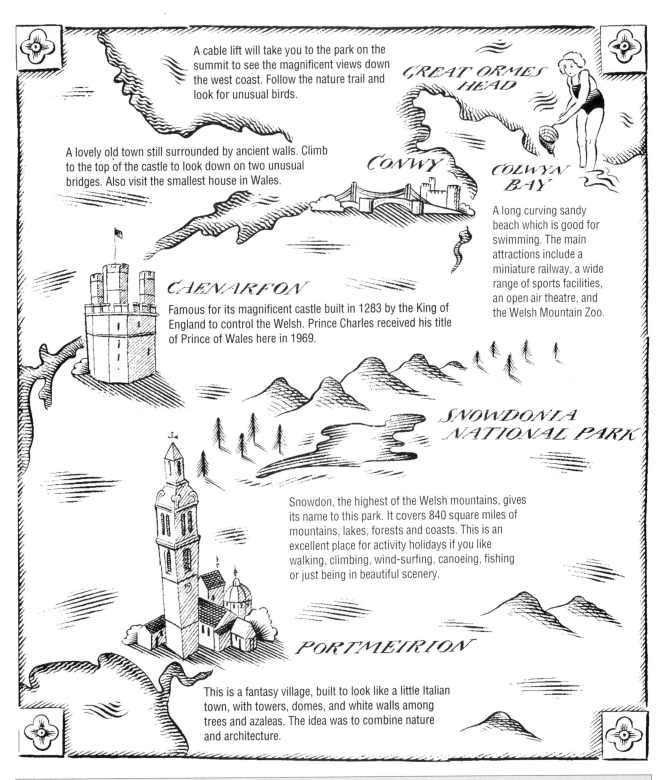

A cable lift will take you to the park on the summit to see the magnificent views down the west coast. Follow the nature trail and look for unusual birds.

GREAT ORMES HEAD

CONWY

A lovely old town still surrounded by ancient walls. Climb to the top of the castle to look down on two unusual bridges. Also visit the smallest house in Wales.

COLWYN BAY

A long curving sandy beach which is good for swimming. The main attractions include a miniature railway, a wide range of sports facilities, an open air theatre, and the Welsh Mountain Zoo.

CAENARFON

Famous for its magnificent castle built in 1283 by the King of England to control the Welsh. Prince Charles received his title of Prince of Wales here in 1969.

SNOWDONIA NATIONAL PARK

Snowdon, the highest of the Welsh mountains, gives its name to this park. It covers 840 square miles of mountains, lakes, forests and coasts. This is an excellent place for activity holidays if you like walking, climbing, wind-surfing, canoeing, fishing or just being in beautiful scenery.

PORTMEIRION

This is a fantasy village, built to look like a little Italian town, with towers, domes, and white walls among trees and azaleas. The idea was to combine nature and architecture.

Homework

1 Draw a map of your country.
2 Mark on it six holiday areas.
3 Make notes about what you can do or see there.

23 Describing Holidays

1 Listen to Ian, Joyce and Pete talking about their holidays to North Wales.

2 Hill-walking is a very popular holiday.

   a Look at the map to see where the best places for hill-walking are.

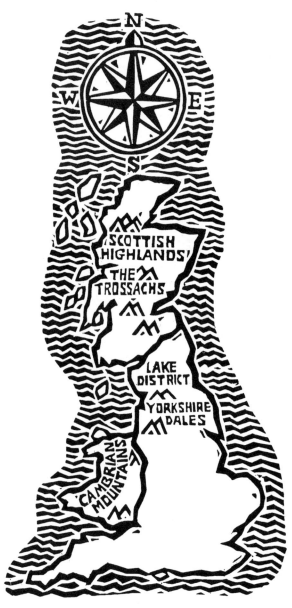

   a Who went:

   (i) to a beautiful village?
   (ii) mountain climbing?
   (iii) on a mountain railway?

   b Did they enjoy their holidays?

b Below is a picture of what you should take when you go hill-walking.

Match the names in the list under the pictures and the items on the pictures.

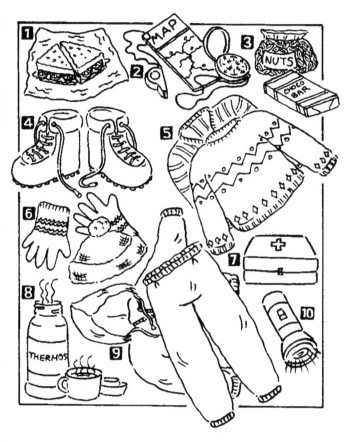

First Aid Kit   Spare Food   Sandwiches   Hot Drink
Hat and Gloves   Map, Compass and Whistle   Torch
Spare Sweaters   Waterproofs   Boots

c What five items do you think are the most important? Give your reasons. Work with three other people and together agree on the five most important things to take.

Item	Reason

3 Listen to Pete and Tim planning a walking weekend in the Lake District (The Lakes).

a Compare your list in **2c** with theirs.

b Here is an official list of what to do when hill-walking.

Did you, Pete or Tim forget anything important?

BEFORE you set out for a day in the mountains, have a good read of these common sense precautions you should follow.

• Wear boots (not shoes) fitted with rubber moutaineering soles.

• Take with you plenty of warm clothing, especially wind and rainproof outer garments (jacket or anorak with a hood, and over-trousers). Never wear jeans: when wet and subjected to a cold wind they are liable to cause 'exposure' (hypothermia) - a dangerous and often fatal condition which can occur at any time of the year, even in summer.

• Carry a map and compass and know how to use them. Also take a whistle, watch, torch, a first aid kit and one or two spare long-sleeved jerseys.

• Take a reserve food supply with you in case of emergency (chocolate, mint cake, biscuits, glucose tablets). A hot drink in a thermos flask is strongly recommended.

HOMEWORK

1 Check Your Vocabulary Quiz.

a What do you wear when it rains in the mountains?
b When your hands are cold, wear _____ .
c Never wear _____ in the mountains.
d When you're tired and cold, it's good to stop for a _____ .
e All walkers carry this to find their directions when they can't see well.
f Excellent emergency food.

2 What is your favourite holiday?
Where is it? What can you do and see there?

24 Writing a Brochure

1 Your local Tourist Information Office is organising a competition.

   a What is the competion about?
   b Who will see these posters?

2 The Local Tourist Board sent you this letter.

Dear Class,

Thank you for your letter asking for details about our 'Design a Poster Competition'. These are the rules:

1 Make our town look interesting.
2 Give basic information about our town.
3 Pictures/photographs can be used.
4 Your poster should be suitable for the general tourist.
5 Four people maximum to design each poster.

The prize is the new book about our town which will be in the shops in six weeks' time.

Good luck! Looking forward to seeing your ideas.

Yours sincerely,

S.T. Thompson

S. T. Thompson
Tourist Information Officer

NATIONAL TOURIST BOARD
COMPETITION

Make our town wealthy

Bring the tourists here!

Design a poster
to use in travel magazines
all over the world.

Write to your local
Tourist Office
for more details.

3 Decide what a tourist would like to see in your town. Below are some ideas.

old buildings of interest
rivers, lakes
shopping centres
restaurants
museums
art galleries
botanical gardens
zoos
parks
modern buildings
cafes

4 Decide what a tourist would like to do in your town. Below are some ideas.

shopping
visiting old buildings
boating on the river
visiting the museum
walking in the park
eating in the restaurants

5 Decide which ideas to use.

6 Design your poster. The tour brochure for York will give you ideas.

Visit York with its 1900 years of history. There's something for everyone here:

- *one of the largest cathedrals in Britain*
- *the Jorvik Viking Centre where you can go back 1,000 years to see the people, houses, food, hear the language and smell old York*
- *the National Railway Museum, one of the best in the world*
- *marvellous shopping in the old narrow streets of the town*
- *excellent places to eat and drink*
- *beautiful walks on the old town walls and by the river*

HOMEWORK

1 Read this tourist brochure description of Saffron Walden.

Saffron Walden *is a small and attractive market town with many interesting old buildings. It is twenty-five kilometres south of Cambridge and about an hour by train from London.*
The town was rich in the middle ages because of the cloth trade. The beautiful wooden house for the Youth Hostel is 14th Century and some of the old pubs go back to the 15th and 16th centuries. The magnificent church, the 12th century castle and the museum are all worth a visit. Tuesdays and Saturdays are market days with a lot to see. The shops are good, parking is easy and there are some excellent tea shops.

2 Write a short description of your town (about 50 words) for a new tourist brochure. Use the description of Saffron Walden to help you.

25 Listening to a Radio Broadcast

1 Answer the questionnaire about your radio listening habits. Complete the column **you**. Then interview someone in your class and complete the column **another student.**

	you	another student
1 When do you listen to the radio?		
2 How many hours a day/ week do you listen?		
3 What do you like to listen to?		
the news		
the weather forecast		
pop music		
classical music		
stories		
talk programmes/interviews		
current affairs		
comedy		
quizzes		

2 a Match these programmes to the types in question 3 of the Questionnaire above.

(i) 9.30 a.m. Breakaway
The holiday programme
(ii) 10.15 p.m. A Book at Bedtime
(iii) 11.30 p.m. A Little Night Music
(iv) 6.25 p.m. Music for Guitar
(v) 2.00 p.m. Woman's Hour
(vi) 4.30 p.m. Science Now
(vii) 10.00 a.m. Out of Order
A quiz about politics.
(viii) 11.00 p.m. The Friday Rock Show
(ix) 9.00 p.m. The Food Programme
(x) 1.00 p.m. The World at One: News
(xi) 1.30 p.m. Sport on 2 at the Open
(xii) 10.30 a.m. Morning Story
I Wish I Had a Parrot

b How many of these radio programmes do you listen to in your own language?

3 Look at the photographs below. What types of programme do you think they describe?

4 Look at what is on Radio 4 today.

a Find programmes to match the pictures in **3**.

b Listen to the radio announcer. Which programmes does she talk about?

RADIO 4

6.30	**The Today Programme**
9.00	**The News**
9.05	**Desert Island Discs:** **Dame Edna Everage chooses the records she would like to have on a desert island.**
9.45	**The Woody Allen Reader: Count Dracula**
10.00	**News around the World**
10.30	**Morning Story: *Dolly's Mother* by Maeve Binchy**
11.00	**The News**
11.05	**My Country, Right or Wrong. Interviews by MI5, MI6 and CIA officers on the Secret Service.**
11.47	**Horrors. It can take four hours to turn an actor into one of the horror film monsters in "Hellraiser II".**
12.00	**You and Yours. How safe is pre-cooked food and should all cars have seat belts in the back?**
12.25	**The Food Programme looks at vegetarianism.**
1.00	**The World at One: News**

---

5 Listen to an interview with Mike Jones on a Music programme.

a What is Mike's job?
b When does he start work?
c When does he finish?
d What kind of music does he like?

6 Mike chooses this song. Listen and fill in the missing words.

MAMA TOLD ME BLUES

1 My mama told me, you'd better be _____ .
    She told me she thought that I would.
    But she just didn't know that
    I _____ could.

2 When I was _____ I travelled away.
    I hit the city - I thought that I'd _____
    But I robbed Jackson's Food Store.
    I couldn't _____ .

3 The police grabbed me before I could _____ .
    They started _____ when they saw my gun.
    Oh I just didn't know that
    Crime was no _____ .

4 I'm stuck in prison, some day I'll be _____ .
    I won't go back to that _____ .
    'Cause I know I'll remember
    What mama _____ me.

Dictionary

hit the city arrive at the city
grab *v* take roughly
stuck *pp* of stick, unable to escape

HOMEWORK

Prepare questions and interview someone in the class. Find out:
1 how he/she spends their day
2 what he/she likes to listen to on the radio or watch on TV
3 what kind of music he/she likes

26 Listening to a Science Fiction Story

1 Find out about the **Bedtime Story** tonight.

   a What is its title?
   b Who wrote it?
   c What kind of story is it?

   romance spy thriller detective
   science fiction adventure

2 Look at the summary of the story and find answers to the following questions.

   a What does the thief try to steal?
   b What is the Siren Goddess?
   c Where is the Siren Goddess?
   d Where is Rawlings?
   e Why is he there?
   f What was his job on Mars?

3 Listen to the description of the Siren Goddess on the news the day it went missing.

   a Fill in the blanks.

> The statue of the Siren Goddess is about _____ inches high and it is made of _____ It is very _____ and very famous. It was kept in the _____ of Meridian City. It was the most _____ in the whole Museum. The _____ on Mars buy _____ of it to take back to Earth.

   b How do you think the thief got the Siren Goddess out of the glass case?

Listen to the story and check

10.15pm The Bedtime Story

Trouble with Time
by ARTHUR C. CLARKE

Read by John Brown

A thief tries to steal the famous statue of the Siren Goddess from the Museum of Meridian City from the planet Mars. Detective Inspector Rawlings tells the story in the departure lounge of the space station of Mars' moon on his way back to Earth.

Mr Maccar, an art dealer and another passenger on the journey to Earth, listens to his story.

4 Danny Weaver is the thief. Look at his plan to steal the Siren Goddess.

Plan
Saturday   Visit museum
16.00   Hide at closing time
24.00   Begin work
Sunday   Cut a statue from case
              Put in copy
              Hide again
Monday   Leave hiding place
10.00   Join visitors
              Leave museum

 Now listen to the story again and answer these questions.

a Tick (✓) the parts of the plan that worked.
b Where was Danny's hotel?
c Where was the Museum?
d What happens every Sunday?

5 Listen to the second part of the story.

a What is the difference between Meridian East and Meridian West?
b What day is it in Meridian East for these days in Meridian West?

Meridian West	Meridian East
Saturday	
Sunday	
Monday	

c What was Danny's big mistake?
d Why are there no prisons on Mars?

6 a Do you think Mr Maccar knows Danny Weaver?

 **b** Listen to the end of the story. Make a note of anything strange about Mr Maccar's voice and face.

HOMEWORK

You work for *Radio Earth*. You've heard the story of the Siren Goddess.

1 Prepare questions to interview Detective Inspector Rawlings when he returns to Earth.

2 Prepare questions to interview Danny Weaver on Mars by satellite radio.

27 Making a Broadcast

In this lesson you are going to prepare and broadcast a short radio programme. The Producer has sent you instructions about what to do.

RADIO LIVE

MEMO

To: News production team

From: The Producer Radio Live

AGENDA

1 Decide what will go into the programme. You can use four of the six topics from **Programme Ideas**.

2 Decide on the order of the programmes.

3 Decide how long each item will be. Maximum four minutes.

4 Decide who will write which news. Maximum four people per group.

5 Decide who is going to be the announcer. The announcer needs to study the **Notes for the Announcer.**

6 Get into groups to prepare your news item. Watch your time! Your controller will tell you how long you have.

7 Decide who will record it.

8 Record your programme.

PROGRAMME IDEAS

National News
Take anything from today's news. Write a short description. You could include the interviews with Detective Inspector Rawlings and Danny Weaver. (Lesson 26 Homework)

Place
Choose an interesting place you've been to in your country or in another country. Talk about it.

Local News
Has anything interesting happened in your town? Anyone famous visiting or going to visit? Write notes about it.

People
Have you seen or met any famous people? Who? When? What happened?

Class News
Has anyone done anything unusual, had a birthday, been somewhere, seen someone? Write notes about it. You could include your homework interview from Lesson 25.

What's on
What's happening in your town this weekend?. Talk about three main events.

NOTES FOR THE ANNOUNCER

You will need to know what the news items are about. Go round and listen to the groups preparing their news.

How to start the programme

This is Radio Live.

Today we will talk about ...

*First of all, the News with May Stuart.
But first of all we will have the News with ...
Our first item is the News with ...*

Linking items of News

*Thank you Jo Brown and Nick Roberts.
That sounds like a really interesting trip.
Now we have ... (next item)*

From London we go to ... Here is ... to talk about it.

That was Eric Williams with a story about ....

Finishing

That is all for today. I hope you can join us again next week.

Homework

Write a short article using information from the interviews from today's programme for the Class Magazine.

28 Using Readers

1 What kind of stories do you like to read:
a most   **b** least

thriller spy stories adventure romance
detective mystery science fiction family
stories horror comedy animal stories real
life stories history

2 Look at the covers of these readers. Guess the
kind of story each is. Match with the names
in **1**.

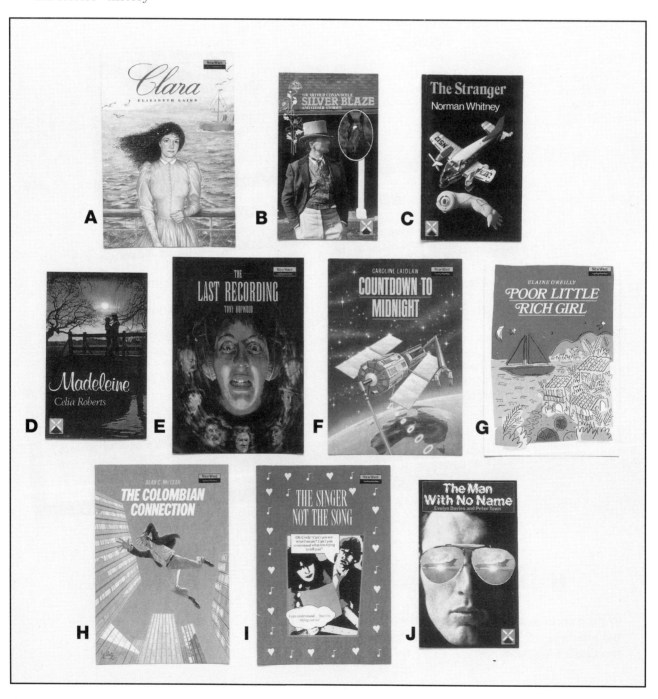

3 Read the description of each story. Match it with its cover.

Sherlock Holmes and Dr Watson help the police with the strange cases of:

The Blue Carbuncle
Two unusual clues for Holmes and Watson to follow - a hat and a goose!
Silver Blaze
A racehorse disappears before an important race. Holmes has to find the horse and solve a murder.
The Six Napoleons
Why is someone smashing statues of Napoleon? What are they looking for?

What was wrong with Paul?
Madelaine thought he loved her.
They were going to get married.
Or were they?

Why didn't he visit her flat?
Not even a phone call.
And why was he seeing the blond girl Sylvie?

Mary started to run towards the aircraft.
Something was wrong..
She saw no one alive or dead and she heard nothing.

What had happened to the passengers and crew of Flight SWY 247?

Cromwell College is no ordinary language school. It hides a dark secret. What are the strange noises in the language laboratory? Why is Max so afraid? Frederick and Beatriz, students at the college, try to help him. But is it too late to solve the mystery?

Clara hates her employers, Mrs Blake and her son Henry. But she doesn't want to lose her job in their home. 'I'll go far away to another country,' she dreams. Then Clara sees an advertisement for jobs in America. 'Everything's going to be wonderful,' she thinks. But can she escape from cruel Henry Blake?

'Drugs are terrible. They kill thousands of people every year. And they ruin the lives of many more people.' Kay Duncan, a young reporter, is determined to expose this evil world. Her investigations lead her from the New York underworld to South America.

'Great news' says Tony, leader of the band, Trio. 'The record company wants us to make our first record.' But why isn't Rob pleased? What happens to the band? Does Cindy love Rob or Tony? And does she know the importance of the song?

Samantha Hamilton lives in Switzerland with her parents. Life is easy but Sam is bored. She doesn't want to go to the opera festival in Salzburg with her father or sail on her Grandpa's yacht again. This summer Sam wants to travel on her own. She's looking for adventure and romance. So she sets off for Sardinia - and finds more than she expects. Suddenly life isn't so easy.

Why does Joe Carter's scientist father move his satellite dish in the middle of the night? Why does he disappear the next day? Will Joe's mother arrive safely in Australia? Joe and his friends follow Professor Carter to Dead Man's Island. But can they stop the war in space?

Woodend was a small, quiet village with no shops, no visitors. Then a stranger came and opened the Corner Shop. That summer visitors came to Woodend. Customers came secretly to the shop. They wanted help and the stranger helped them.

4 What are the stories about? Copy the box below and fill in the answers.

Title	Main characters	Job	Place of story	Kind of story
eg Colombian Connection	Kay Duncan	Reporter	New York, South America	Adventure about drugs

5 Which story would you like to read?

HOMEWORK

Look at the picture from the beginning of the detective story *The Blue Carbuncle.*

a   What is the man in the middle carrying?
b   What is he doing?
c   What happens?
d   What time of year is it?

29 Reading a Detective Story

1 Look at the first two pages of the story of *The Blue Carbuncle* to check your answers in your homework (Lesson 28).

THE BLUE CARBUNCLE

1   A Hat and a Goose

It was two days after Christmas. I decided to visit my friend Sherlock Holmes, the famous private detective.
When I entered the sitting-room, Holmes was lying on the sofa. He was smoking his pipe. Beside the sofa was a chair. A hat was hanging from the back of the chair. The hat looked old and dirty.
Holmes was staring at the hat.
'Are you busy this morning, Holmes?' I asked.
'No, Watson,' said Holmes. 'I'm glad you've come. Look at this hat. It's very interesting.'
'Why is it interesting?' I asked. 'Who does the hat belong to?'
'I don't know,' replied Holmes. 'But Peterson, the porter who looks after this apartment, found it. He also found a goose with the hat.'
'A hat and a goose!' I cried. 'How strange. How did Peterson find these things?'
'The night before Christmas,' Holmes said, 'Peterson went to a party. After the party, he walked home along Tottenham Court Road. A tall man was walking in front of him. This man was carrying a large white goose over his shoulder.'
'Suddenly,' Holmes continued, ' a group of rough young men appeared. They tried to attack the tall man. Perhaps they wanted to steal the goose. The tall man raised his walking stick. But the stick hit a shop window behind him. The broken glass fell on the pavement with a loud crash.'
'The tall man became frightened,' Holmes went on. 'He dropped the goose and ran away. Peterson went towards the young men. When they saw him, they also ran away. Perhaps they thought Peterson was a policeman.'
'What did Peterson do then?' I asked.
'He brought the hat and the goose to me on Christmas morning,' replied Holmes. 'A label was tied to the goose's leg. This label said "For Mrs Henry Baker." And the initials "H.B." were inside the hat.'
'So the owner of the hat must be Mr Henry Baker,' I said.
'And the goose was probably a present for his wife. By the way, Holmes - where is the goose?'
'Peterson and his family are eating it now,' Holmes replied.
Suddenly the door opened and a man rushed in. It was Peterson. He was very excited.
'The goose, Mr Holmes! The goose!' he cried.
We stared at Peterson in astonishment.
'What's happened to the goose?' asked Holmes.
'Look, sir!' said Peterson. 'See what my wife has found inside the goose.'
Peterson held out his hand. In the palm of his hand, I saw a beautiful blue jewel. The jewel shone and sparkled with brilliant lights.
'What is it, Holmes?' I asked. 'Is it a diamond?'
Holmes leaned forward excitedly.
'No, Watson,' he said. 'It isn't a diamond. It's the Blue Carbuncle.'
'The Blue Carbuncle!' I said. 'What's that?'

2 Who's who? Match the name and the description.

Sherlock Holmes   *a porter in the flats where Sherlock Holmes lives*
Peterson   *a famous detective in London*
Henry Baker   *Sherlock Holmes' friend*
Dr Watson   *the tall man who lost a goose*

3 Check the clues so far. Mark each clue True (T) or False (F).

a Peterson saw a tall man carrying a chicken.
b A group of young men attacked the tall man.
c The tall man broke a shop window.
d He dropped the chicken and walked away.
e The young men saw Peterson and ran.
f Peterson picked up the goose and hat.
g He took them to Dr Watson.
h Peterson ate the goose for his Christmas dinner.

4 Sherlock Holmes had this newspaper cutting about the Blue Carbuncle.

a Where was the jewel?
b When was it stolen?
c Who discovered the robbery?

The Times   December 21st 1893

JEWEL ROBBERY AT THE HOTEL COSMOPOLITAN BLUE CARBUNCLE STOLEN

The Countess of Morcar's famous jewel, the Blue Carbuncle, was stolen this afternoon. The robbery took place at the Hotel Cosmopolitan, where the Countess was staying.

The robbery was discovered by Mr James Ryder, under-manager of the hotel. Mr Ryder found that someone had broken into the Countess's room.

The Countess kept the Blue Carbuncle in a jewel-box in her desk. The jewel-box was empty and the Blue Carbuncle had disappeared.

5 Sherlock Holmes makes notes about the mystery so far.

> Blue Carbuncle found _____
> Peterson got goose _____
> Blue Carbuncle stolen _____
> Henry Baker attacked _____

a Put the facts in order.
b Add the dates when they happened.

6 Did Henry Baker steal the Blue Carbuncle? Sherlock Holmes sends this advertisement to all the evening newspapers.

> **Found in Tottenham Court Road on Christmas Eve - a goose and black hat. Mr Henry Baker can have these things if he comes to 221B Baker Street at 6.30 in the evening.**

7 Mr Baker comes to see Sherlock Holmes and gives him some new clues to follow. The clues give information about the goose and where it came from.

a Look at the clues.

ALFA INN
Special Prices For Your Christmas Goose
Pay 2 pence a week from
1st October - 24th December
Take your goose home for Christmas

Accounts Book Mrs Oakshott Brixton Road
22nd December | 5 Geese sold to Mr Breckinridge, Covent Garden Market

Accounts Book Mr Breckinridge Covent Garden Market
23rd December | 20 Geese sold to Mr Windigate, Manager of Alfa Inn

b Match the owners of the goose and the dates.
Mr Breckinridge   Mr Henry Baker
Mrs Oakshott   Mr Windigate
Up to 22nd December   22nd-23rd December
23rd-24th December   24th December

8 Sherlock Holmes and Dr Watson are in Covent Garden Market when something happens. Read the story and follow Sherlock Holmes.

Suddenly we heard angry voices behind us. A man was standing in front of Breckinridge's stall. This man was small with a sharp, pointed face. He was arguing loudly with Breckinridge. 'One of those geese was mine,' the man was saying. 'Tell me who you sold it to.'
'I'll tell you nothing!' shouted Breckinridge. 'Don't come back here again. Don't ask me any more questions about those geese. Now go away or I'll call the police!'
The man turned and ran off down the dark street.
'Come on, Watson,' said Holmes. 'Let's follow that man!'
We ran after the man. When we reached him, Holmes laid his hand on the man's shoulder. The man sprang round. His face was white with fear.
'Who are you? What do you want?' he whispered.
'Excuse me,' said Holmes, 'but I think you're interested in some geese. Or rather one special goose. A goose that Breckinridge bought from Mrs Oakshott of Brixton Road.'
'Oh sir,' said the man. 'I'm very interested in finding this goose. Can you help me?'
'Perhaps I can,' answered Holmes. 'But first you must tell me your name.'
'My name is James Ryder,' said the man.
'James Ryder!' repeated Holmes. 'I know that name. Yes, I remember. It was in the newspaper story about the jewel robbery. You're the under-manager of the Hotel Cosmopolitan. The Blue Carbuncle was stolen from that hotel. Come with us, Mr Ryder. I have some questions to ask

What do you think happened?

9 Read the beginning of James Ryder's story.

'I am Under-Manager at the Hotel Cosmopolitan,' said Ryder. 'The Countess of Morcar came to stay at the hotel and I became friendly with the Countess's maid. The maid told me the Countess owned a famous jewel. The jewel was called the Blue Carbuncle. The maid also told me where the jewel was kept. It was kept in a desk in the Countess's bedroom.'
'I decided to steal the Blue Carbuncle,' Ryder went on. 'One afternoon, I saw the Countess leave the hotel. I had keys to all the rooms in the hotel. I went into the Countess's bedroom and opened the desk. I found a jewel-box in the desk. Inside the jewel-box was the Blue Carbuncle.'
Ryder stopped talking for a moment. Then he continued his story.
'I took out the jewel and left the empty jewel-box on the desk. I left the door of the Countess's room open. Then I called the police. The police came at once. I told them that someone had broken into the Countess's room. When the Countess returned, she found that the Blue Carbuncle was missing.'
'Then what happened?' asked Holmes.
'The police didn't think I was the thief,' Ryder went on. 'But I was getting very worried. The Blue Carbuncle was still in my pocket.'

HOMEWORK

Continue James Ryder's story. How did the Blue Carbuncle get into Mrs Oakshott's goose?

I decided to leave the hotel as quickly as possible. I went ...

30 Writing a Story

1 In this lesson you will write a chain story using ideas from the pictures. A chain story works like this:

You and your friend begin the story and write the first paragraph. You then give it to another group to read and they write the second paragraph. This continues with a group writing each paragraph. Look what happens in the story below.

story | para 1 You → para 2 Group 2 → para 3 Group 3

story | para 1 Group 3 → para 2 You → para 3 Group 2

story | para 1 Group 2 → para 2 Group 3 → para 3 You

2 Read about *The Last Recording*.

The Last Recording

Cromwell College is no ordinary language school. It hides a dark secret. What are the strange noises in the language laboratory? Why is Max so afraid? Frederick and Beatriz, students at the college, try to help him. But is it too late to solve the mystery of The Last Recording?

3 Read the beginning of the story.

Frederick, a student from Switzerland, has just arrived in England to study English in a language school. This is what happens when he arrives.

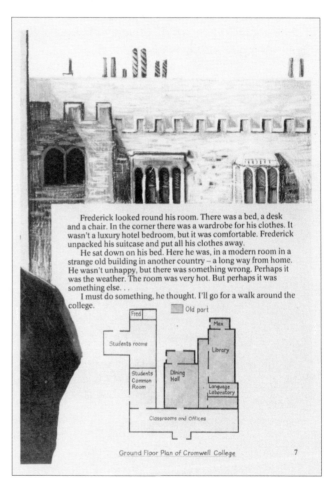

Frederick looked round his room. There was a bed, a desk and a chair. In the corner there was a wardrobe for his clothes. It wasn't a luxury hotel bedroom, but it was comfortable. Frederick unpacked his suitcase and put all his clothes away.

He sat down on his bed. Here he was, in a modern room in a strange old building in another country – a long way from home. He wasn't unhappy, but there was something wrong. Perhaps it was the weather. The room was very hot. But perhaps it was something else. . .

I must do something, he thought. I'll go for a walk around the college.

Ground Floor Plan of Cromwell College   7

4 Continue the story.

a   Where does Frederick go?
b   Who does he meet?
c   What happens?

5 Give your story to another group. Continue their story. Use these pictures for ideas if you wish.

6 Give your story to another group. Finish their story. Use these pictures for ideas if you want.

HOMEWORK

Write a review of the story you liked most. Follow this review of *The Blue Carbuncle*.

Title *The Blue Carbuncle*
Author *Sir Arthur Conan Doyle*

This is a detective story about Sherlock Holmes. A famous jewel disappears and Sherlock Holmes finds it in a goose. I enjoyed the mystery. I thought Mr Baker was the thief at first; after that I didn't know. The English was not too difficult and I read it quickly.

Teacher's Notes

The following notes are intended to help the teacher prepare the activities and provide some further suggestions.

UNIT 1 PEOPLE

Aims

- Introducing the idea of integrated skills activities with one skill helping the other (eg reading as an aid to listening).
- Getting to know more about one another.

LESSON 1
Describing Your Room

1a can be done as a brainstorm on the board or in groups/pairs to revise furniture vocabulary. **1c** checks on the vocabulary in addition to preparing the learner for the listening. **2** is also dual purpose; it is a pre-listening activity and revises colours. Bring some coloured objects or pictures to the class to help with this.

LESSON 2
Talking about Your Favourite Day

1a is a warm-up activity. **1b** and **2** practise scanning and intensive reading skills. The learner can do this best alone first and then check in pairs for oral practice. **3** and **4** practise listening. Play the tape completely for **3** and check the answers before playing the tape again for **4**. **5** is a writing activity which prepares the learner for oral practice in **6**.

LESSON 3
Describing Personalities

Detailed questionnaires on finding out about one another are provided to build confidence and allow for maximum guided oral practice. If preferred, the learners can provide their own questions; a brainstorm on the board will give them an idea of what to do. The final aim is to have profiles of the individual members of the class which can be put on the classroom wall as a display.

UNIT 2 LANGUAGE LEARNING

Aims

- Finding out about different ways of learning languages.
- Deciding how you learn a foreign language best.
- Learning more about vocabulary strategies and reading skills.

LESSON 4
Comparing Study Habits

Introduce the topic by explaining that the lesson is going to look the different ways there are to study successfully. If you have an adult class, begin by having a chat about how the class studied when they were at school/college and if their study techniques are any different now. Allow time for discussion of

1b and 3 in pairs or groups before having a report back session with the whole class.

LESSON 5
Ideas for Vocabulary

Briefly revise some of the ideas from Lesson 4. The main focus in this lesson is intensive listening with tasks to help this. It is important that the learners go through the questions in pairs before they hear the tape. Problem vocabulary like *long* and *short-term memory* can be discussed here. They then listen to the tape to confirm their predictions.

Here are some suggested guidelines for a vocabulary notebook which you could discuss with the class.

1

English	Translation

2

New Word	Example	Translation

3 New words and a diagram (eg for a lexical set on furniture). No translation.

4 Use the new words in a short paragraph and underline them (eg describing the colours in their room). No translation.

LESSON 6
Reading in a Foreign Language

This lesson raises awareness of different reading techniques and practises prediction, reading for general gist and more intensive reading with dictionary work. Discuss the dictionary exercise, particularly how not to go for the first definition in a dictionary. You may find your learners need more practice of dictionary skills.

LESSON 7
Describing Clothes

1 gives further practice of prices and revises clothes vocabulary. **3** is intensive reading and extends clothes

UNIT 3 AUCTION

Aims

- Describing physical objects.
- Practising numbers and prices.
- Extending clothes vocabulary, in particular adjectives for describing clothes, as well as providing an opportunity for oral practice. Remind the learners to practise their reading skills (see Lesson 6), they should not try to understand every word.

LESSON 8
Describing Objects

2 introduces the language of the auction through reading about the objects for sale in a catalogue and matching their descriptions to the photographs. In doing this the learner is being exposed to a wide range of language with written and visual prompts to aid the listening. In addition the learner is revising adjective order. In **3** the learners listen while looking at the catalogue at the same time. Their task is to recognise the items being described and understand the prices. They could then check these in pairs after the auction, to practise talking about prices. **4** and **5** practise adjective order.

LESSON 9
Class Auction

The main aim is to hold a class auction to provide intensive practice in describing objects and giving prices both orally and in writing. It is important for the learners to bring in some objects. If they don't, they can imagine something or draw it and then write the catalogue description. The notes in the students' section are detailed. There are three main sections to the lesson: Making the Catalogue (**1**); Pre-auction (**2** and **3**) ;the Auction (**4**). Make sure they understand the instructions for each section before they begin.

UNIT 4 A WEEKEND AWAY

Aims

- Making choices about a holiday.
- Describing food.

LESSON 10
Choosing a Weekend Break

This lesson focuses on different types of reading texts: a formal letter, instructions and tourist brochures. 3 involves intensive reading. **4** begins with scanning followed by more intensive reading for vocabulary skills.

LESSON 11
Choosing Leisure Activities

1 to **4** are fairly short, preparing the learners with the vocabulary and some ideas for the oral work in **5**. **5a** is group work on decision making.

LESSON 12
Describing Food and Drink

The vocabulary of food is the main focus here, with reading practice of a restaurant menu board and an informal letter. This is followed by writing an informal letter with guidance. Encourage discussion as much as possible in **1** to **3** and **5**.

Note:

Shepherd's Pie - beef and vegetables baked in the oven with a covering of mashed potatoes.

Yorkshire Pudding - a mixture of flour, milk, a little fat, salt and eggs, baked at high temperature and traditionally served with roast beef.

Mint Sauce - fresh mint leaves, finely chopped, in vinegar.

UNIT 5 EXHIBITION

Aims

- Introducing ways of describing physical appearance.
- Introducing lay-out of informal letters.
- Writing a short letter describing yourself.
- Developing character description.

LESSON 13
Describing People

The intensive listening of the waxworks descriptions in **4** is the main focus of this lesson. **1** is an introduction to the topic. The reading in **2** is preparation for the listening and introduces some of the language of describing people. Begin **4** with pairwork or groupwork in the prediction stages, **a** and **b**, and in the checking stage **d**. The class may need to listen to parts of the tape several times.

You may wish to do the homework task in class as a guessing game (see notes for Lesson 14).

LESSON 14
Describing Character

You could begin with the homework task from Lesson 13. If each homework description is read aloud, the class can guess who it is describing (listening practice). Alternatively, for reading and writing practice, the written homework descriptions can be circulated and read in groups, perhaps with a group of four learners exchanging descriptions with another group of four and writing who they think is being described in each description.

1 to **6** are best done as pair work to encourage more oral work.

You may wish to do the homework task in class as described above.

LESSON 15
Pen-friends

If your learners would like pen-friends, useful sources are 'Penfriends' in *BBC English* and 'Contacts and Exchanges' in *Practical English Teacher*. They could send their advertisements to a real source.

The layout of the letter in **4** is important. Discuss differences between layout of an English letter and that of their country.

UNIT 6 FESTIVALS

Aims

- Developing skills for following spoken and written narrative.
- Describing how a simple recipe is prepared.

LESSON 16
Hallowe'en

Discuss the introduction, *Hallowe'en* and explain any vocabulary eg *the dead would rise from their graves, spirits, ghosts*. You could bring in some ghostly music to set the scene.

The listening is in two sections, **5** being more guided than **6**. Both practise listening for specific details.

LESSON 17
Ghost Stories

Introduce the concept of Superstitions. For example, in Britain, Friday 13th is an unlucky day; many people won't travel on that day. Ask the class for similar superstitions from their own country.

In **1** Pre-teach *cemetery, ladder* and *UFO (Unidentified Flying Object)* and link this up with the discussion on superstitions. **2** practises listening for specific information. **3** prepares the vocabulary needed for the story in **4**.

LESSON 18
Traditional Recipes

Encourage discussion in **1** to find out about other customs.

Note: *Lent* in Christian countries was traditionally 40 days of fasting (not eating rich food like eggs, butter, sugar, milk, meat) before Easter, the day when Christ rose from the dead. Pancake Day is the day before Lent begins, when the rich food had to be finished.

A follow-up to this lesson could be group work preparing descriptions of customs in their country for a poster display, for example:

```
name of custom
date
what we do
what we eat
```

Or you could have a competition for a new international festival poster, for example:

Peace Day	
Date	15th August
Food	Bread and water
What happens	People sing peace songs They carry an olive branch

UNIT 7 MAGAZINE

Aims

- Preparing a class magazine.
- Interviewing and collecting information.
- Reading different types of magazine articles.

These lessons cover a variety of topics common in magazines with the aim that the class write their own magazine in Lesson 21.

LESSON 19
Preparing a Health Questionnaire

1 and **2** can be done in pairs. **3** and **4** can be followed with pair work to encourage as much discussion as possible.

LESSON 20
Reading Factual Information

1 and **4** can be done in pairs for oral practice.

LESSON 21
Making a Magazine

The homework for Lessons 19 and 20 can be used here. The class will need to select the items they like best. Ideas are given for what to include in the magazine, but encourage other ideas from the class to make it their magazine.

Depending on the facilities available, the magazine can be done as a wall display, small book or on a word processor (obviously this is more time-consuming).

UNIT 8 TOURIST INFORMATION

Aims

- Describing places.
- Developing intensive reading and listening skills.
- Writing a simple tourist brochure.

LESSON 22
Reading Holiday Brochures

This recycles some of the language of Unit 4 and develops the use of adjectives for descriptions. The skills focus of this lesson is scanning for specific information. The homework can be discussed in class. If you have a multi-lingual group, learners of one nationality may like to work on this together.

LESSON 23
Describing Holidays

The three short interviews and one longer one form the focus of this lesson on developing a holiday activity in more detail. The short interviews are not intended to be exploited beyond **1** (listening for gist). **3** will require more intensive listening, the tape will possibly have to be played several times.

LESSON 24
Writing a Brochure

Writing and oral skills are developed in this lesson as is the language of description. Pair or group work will be needed to brainstorm ideas for **3** and **4**. The poster in **6** can also be done in a group. Pair work is helpful to prepare ideas for the homework. The writing skills are those of layout and extended notes.

UNIT 9 RADIO STATION

Aims

- Preparing a Radio Programme
- Developing intensive and extensive listening skills.

LESSON 25
Listening to a Radio Broadcast

Intensive listening to radio programmes is the main focus of this lesson. The learners could read the song in **6** before they hear it and try to guess the missing words. There is a mini-dictionary to help them with the difficult words.

At the end of the lesson, prepare the class for making their own programmes in Lesson 27 and ask them to start thinking of ideas.

LESSON 26
Listening to a Science Fiction Story

A variety of listening skills is practised in order to understand this story: prediction, listening for specific information and deduction.

The class may need to hear parts of the tape more than once.

LESSON 27
Making a Broadcast

You will need a blank tape and a tape recorder. If you do not have these, do it 'live'.

To prepare a radio programme properly could take much longer than the forty-five minutes allowed for this lesson. For this reason, the lesson is fairly guided and the learners are not expected to go into very much detail. If you have more time, you can easily expand the ideas and allow the learners more freedom to choose what they want to include.

The principal aim of the lesson is to give the learners a chance to exchange ideas, make decisions and gain confidence in using English to produce an item of news. They will make mistakes, but it is more important for them to have a sense of achievement from preparing something like this than to be worried about how accurate their English is.

Procedure

1 Briefly introduce the idea of making a radio programme.
2 Tell the class that the details are in their books and ask them to read the Memo from the Producer quickly to see what has to be done.
3 While they are reading, put the headings shown below on the board. These are the same ones as in the Programmes Ideas in the students' section. The question mark is for their own ideas. For example, there is nothing on sport.

	What	Who
National News		
Local News	People	
Class News, etc.		
?		

4 Ask the learners to talk in pairs for a couple of minutes for ideas on what to do using the Programme Ideas.

5 Brainstorm their ideas. Use your headings on the board to decide what to do and who will prepare it.
6 Go through the Agenda item by item. You are the Controller so be very careful about how much time they have to prepare and how much time they can allocate for the broadcast.
7 When they are in groups, go round and make sure they all know what to do. Help any weak groups and check the announcer understands his/her notes. This is a time when you could be making a note of their language mistakes for correction later.
8 Fifteen minutes before the end of the lesson, announce that they are about to go on air, ask the announcer to take his/her place beside the microphone.
9 Record.
10 Get feedback on how they felt and comment on their language.

UNIT 10 A GOOD READ

Aims

- Developing intensive and extensive reading skills.
- Becoming familiar with guided readers.
- Writing a simple story.

Use this unit to encourage the use of readers in English. If you have a class or school library, introduce the learners to it. Get a copy of *Silver Blaze*, which contains the Sherlock Holmes story in Lesson 29 and *The Last Recording*, used in Lesson 30, to find out what really happens.

LESSON 28
Using Readers

1 revises the vocabulary the learners need to talk about books. In **2** they use these terms to predict types of story from their covers. It does not matter if their predictions are not correct. For example, **2b** *Silver Blaze and Other Stories* looks from the cover to be an historical story or one about animals. If the learners have heard of Conan Doyle, they will guess 'detective'. At this stage accept all possible answers, provided the learners can give a good reason. In **3** the learners match the descriptions to their covers. The correct answers are in the Key, but other answers are also acceptable if the reason is a good one. The important point is that the learners are thinking about what they are reading and any disagreements give an opportunity for discussion.

LESSON 29
Reading a Detective Story

A Sherlock Holmes short story is covered in this lesson. The reading skills practised are scanning for specific information, deduction and prediction.

LESSON 30
Writing a Story

Make sure the class understands what the chain story in **1** is. As it is a kind of game, it is best written in pairs. The pictures are to help with ideas, but you may find you have some learners who want to develop their own story without these pictures.

Key

UNIT 1 PEOPLE

LESSON 1
Describing Your Room

1 a *Suggested answers*
   chair/sofa picture/poster lights book-shelves/cases
   desk rugs/carpets television plant fire curtains/
   blind cushion boxes
   c chair/sofa picture/poster television plant fire

2 b futon, blind and spot-lights: red
   Greek cushion: red
   rug: red, maroon and blue

3 Crete

4 A futon comes from Japan. English people have
   sofas.

5 diagonal zig-zag cube/box octagonal

LESSON 2
Talking About Your Favourite Day

1 a 1 neck 2 shoulders 3 ribs 4 back-bone 5 hips
   6 hands 7 right leg 8 feet 9 left arm 10 skull
   b no

2 9.00 **a** 11.00 **a** 12.30 **b** 3.00 **c** evening **c**

3 a Saturday
   b Anna works in a hotel as a receptionist
   c when she goes out in the evening

4 8.00-100 write essays
   2.00 fall asleep
   5.00 have shower
   9.00 watch band

UNIT 2 LANGUAGE LEARNING

LESSON 5
Ideas for Vocabulary

1a 2b 3a 4b 5b 6a 7a, b or c 8b 9a

LESSON 6
Reading in a Foreign Language

3 a something about a young person
d Adragon Eastwood DeMello/an 11 year-old boy.
   He is going to study astrophysics or particle
   physics/study at Oxford, London or Cambridge.
   He is the youngest person in the world to have a
   university degree in Mathematics.

5 sleep/rest turned/switched/put good/use full
   think/guess asleep eyes

UNIT 3 AUCTION

LESSON 7
Describing Clothes

1 a £55.93
   b it wasn't bad value / one of my best buys / it is so
   cheap / a bit of a bargain

3 The photos match the descriptions as follows:
   1f 2d 3f 4a 5h 6g 7b 8c 9i

LESSON 8
Describing Objects

3

item		starting price	finishing price
1	long knife	£20	£30
2	round plate	£5	£10
3	antelope	£3	£10
4	map	£20	did not sell

4 11 a small red wine glass
   12 a square wooden box
   13 a long silver necklace
   14 a small Swiss army knife

5 The treasure is in **4d**

UNIT 4 A WEEKEND AWAY

LESSON 10
Choosing a Weekend Break

4

	Sherwood Forest Holiday Village	Crown Hotel London
stay in a villa	✓	
watch colour TV	✓	✓
have a lake outside your bedroom	✓	
play badminton	✓	
go shopping for antiques		
go on a boat trip		✓
have your own bathroom		✓
relax in a quiet place	✓	
stay in a hotel		✓
see famous 'people' and places		✓
go swimming	✓	

5 popular - everyone likes it   leisurely - relaxing
marvellous - very good   antique - old object
en suite facilities - bathroom next to bedroom
giant - very large dome - a round shape
fully equipped - kitchen which has everything
fitted - carpet from wall to wall

LESSON 11
Choosing Leisure Activities

3 **a** In a holiday village **b** Her friends told her to go.
There is a lot to do for small children
c 18 months old **d** swimming, tennis, hiring
bicycles, jacuzzis **e** jacuzzi

4 Joanna - swimming pool Nicky - lying under trees
with a drink Jeff - wind-surfing

LESSON 12
Describing Food and Drink

1 **a** Hamburgers - USA spaghetti bolognaise - Italy
paella - Spain curry - India crepes Suzettes -
France cheese fondue - Switzerland
fish and chips - Britain chili con carne - Mexico
sweet and sour pork - China pizza - Italy
sate - Indonesia moussaka - Greece
b coke - USA green tea - China /Japan warm beer
Britain sake - Japan port - Portugal cognac -
France tea with milk - Britain whisky - Scotland
Champagne - France vodka - Russia sherry - Spain
c fish and chips bacon and eggs cereal fruit cake
marmalade puddings custard roast meat mint
sauce
3 *Suggested Answers*
Breakfast: cereal toast and marmalade bacon and
eggs tea
Lunch: look at ideas on the board in **2**
Supper: fish and chips cold meat and salad roast
meat and vegetables

UNIT 5 EXHIBITION

LESSON
13 Describing People

1 **a** London **b** Over 200 years **c** famous people
past and present **d** people all ages and all
nationalities **e** 2 million people per year
2 Hitchcock: **b d f i**
Bowie: **a c e g h j**

3

Hitchcock	Bowie	
height	short	medium height
hair		thick shiny hair
eyes	dark brown	blue
clothes	dark suit	light suit, blue neck-tie

4 **a** 1 - JR   2 - Boy George   3 - Picasso
4 - Agatha Christie
c 1 - JR   2 - Picasso   3 - Agatha Christie
4 - Boy George
d JR - smart suit tie belt cowboy hat
looks menacing(frightening)
Picasso - old man big mouth keen eyes bald
check trousers
Agatha Christie - large legs glasses dress pearl
necklace
Boy George - long hair(braided) hat big shoes,
boots make-up

LESSON 14
Describing Character

1 JR and Agatha Christie
4 hard-working - 3 kind - 6 shy - 8 honest - 2
friendly - 1 serious - 7 clever - 5 happy - 4
amusing - 9
5 easy-going - hard-working cheerful - serious
unkind - kind angry - happy unfriendly - friendly
self-confident - shy dishonest - honest stupid -
clever boring - amusing

UNIT 6 FESTIVALS

LESSON 16
Hallowe'en

2 **a** - 2   **b** - 1   **c** - 3
3 **a** Treats: apples nuts chocolates sweets
c the children cut his roses
e to carry the 'treats'
5 c g b d a e f
6 The children are wearing witches/ghosts clothes,
pretending to be ghosts.
7 **a** They paint their faces and put on old clothes,
curtains or shawls.
b They visit the neighbours and play 'Trick or
Treat'.
8 Hallowe'en words: apple pumpkin face trick
treats witches sweet nut ghost

LESSON 17
Ghost Stories

2 **a** T **b** T **c** T **d** F **e** F **f** T **g** T **h** F **i** F **j** T
3 **a** 1 tail 2 claws 3 wing 4 beak 5 head
c tiny little large enormous gigantic

Homework
a They went into the office after 6 o'clock, lit the gas,
locked the doors and windows and put chalk on the
floor.
b sleepy/bored
c The doors and windows blew open and the lights
went out.
d A noise like the beating of gigantic wings.
e A large shape.

f The doors and windows locked again and the lights came on.

g The claw prints of an enormous bird.

h They ran away.

2 **a** haunted **b** locked **c** bored **d** suddenly
e terrifying **f** beating

UNIT 7 MAGAZINE

LESSON 19

Preparing a Health Questionnaire

3 **a** Fat and overweight.
b She smoked, ate unhealthy food and did not have time for big meals.
c Healthy food: brown bread, fish, vegetables and salads.
d She became thinner - from size 14 in clothes to size 10.
e High calorie: cakes, chocolates, cola. Low calorie: salads, vegetables, fish.

4 **a** 100 years **b** It is low calorie **c** They drink 2-4 cups of rum and they smoke 40-60 cigarettes a day.
d Because of their herbal tea.

LESSON 20

Reading Factual Information

1 **Basic facts**
a 21,000 **b** 1,469 **c** 9.30a.m. **d** 26 miles
e £9 million **f** charity **g** ballerina, house, elephant, cake on head

2 **People facts**
a Danish **b** 2hrs 25 mins 41 secs **c** 15 mins 21 secs
d 82 **e** 4 hrs 7 mins **f** tears, others helped
g Maisie Williams

3 **a** Cuddles
b I'm not sure, more than £20 million.
c From outer space.
d I think dancing is the most wonderful thing of all time.
e Yes. I'm very fond of children.
f Well, I suppose you might think it's strange to sleep in an oxygen tent ...

4 **Crossword**

Across	Down
1 snack	2 calories
6 fond	3 healthy
7 ate	4 runner
8 energy	5 space
	9 menu

UNIT 8 TOURIST INFORMATION

LESSON 22

Reading Holiday Brochures

1 A - 5 B - 6 C - 4 D - 2 E - 3 F - 1
2 **b** Scotland - walking Lake District - climbing
Wales - camping Cornwall - beaches
Norfolk - boating London - theatres

3 **a** Colwyn Bay **b** Conwy **c** Great Ormes Head
d Portmeirion **e** Snowonia **f** Colwyn Bay
4 **a** highest **b** excellent **c** famous **d** fantasy
e miniature **f** magnificent **g** unusual

LESSON 23

Describing Holidays

1 **a** (i) Ian (ii) Pete (iii) Joyce
2 **b** 1 Sandwiches 2 Compass and whistle
3 Spare Food 4 Boots 5 Spare Sweaters
6 Hat and Gloves 7 First Aid Kit 8 Hot Drink
9 Water Proofs 10 Torch

Homework

1 **a** rainproof outer garments anorak waterproofs jacket
b gloves **c** jeans **d** hot drink **e** a compass
f chocolate mint cake

UNIT 9 RADIO STATION

LESSON 25

Listening to a Radio Broadcast

2 **a** (i) interviews/talk programme (ii) story
(iii) music (iv) music (v) interviews/talk programme (vi) science (vii) quiz/current affairs
(viii) music (ix) interviews (x) News (xi) sport
(xii) story

4 **a** Desert Island Discs The Woody Allen Reader
My Country Right or Wrong
b 9.00 news Desert Island Discs Woody Allen
Reader My Country Right or Wrong Horrors

5 **a** a sports teacher **b** 3.30 **c** 9.30 **d** Blues

6 **Verse 1**: good never **Verse 2**: sixteen stay pay
Verse 3: run shooting fun **Verse 4**: free city told

LESSON 26

Listening to a Science Fiction Story

1 **a** Trouble with Time **b** Arthur C. Clarke **c** science fiction

2 **a** a famous statue/the Siren Goddess **b** a statue
c in the Museum of Meridian City on Mars
d On Mars' moon's space station **e** going back to Earth **f** we don't know

3 eight sandstone old Museum valuable tourists copies

4 **a** Everything worked until 'Sunday' morning.
b in Meridian West
c in Meridian East
d the museum is closed

5 **a** one day

b **Meridian West**   **Meridian East**

Meridian West	Meridian East
Saturday	Friday
Sunday	Saturday
Monday	Sunday

c He forgot about the date-line. It was only Saturday in the Museum.

d There is very little crime. Everyone is searched when they leave the city.

6 a Yes

b Mr Maccar's voice was as cold as ice. He had a strange look on his face.

UNIT 10 A GOOD READ

LESSON 28
Using Readers

2 **A** - adventure/romance **B** detective (could be animal/history from the cover) **C** adventure/thriller/mystery **D** romance **E** horror/mystery **F** science fiction **G** family/adventure **H** adventure/mystery/thriller **I** romance **J** mystery

3 1 **B** 2 **D** 3 **J** 4 **E** 5 **A** 6 **H** 7 **I** 8 **G** 9 **F** 10 **C**

4

Title of book	Main characters	Job	Place of story	What kind of story
The Colombian Connection	Kay Duncan	reporter	New York South America	adventure about drugs
Countdown to Midnight	Joe Carter	student	Australia	science-fiction space war
Poor Little Rich Girl	Samantha Hamilton	student	Switzerland Sardinia	adventure romance
The Last Recording	Max Frederick Beatriz	teacher student student	language school	mystery
The Singer not the Song	Tony Rob Cindy	singers		romance and mystery
Clara	Clara	works in a house	England?	adventure?
Madeleine	Madeleine Paul			romance
Silver Blaze	Sherlock Holmes Dr Watson	detectives	England	detective
The Man with No Name	Mary	?	aeroplane	mystery
The Stranger	the stranger	shop owner	Woodend	mystery

Homework

a a stick/a goose **b** hitting someone **c** answer in next lesson **d** winter

LESSON 29
Reading a Detective Story

2 Sherlock Holmes: a famous detective Peterson: a porter in the flats where Sherlock Holmes lives Henry Baker: the tall man who lost a goose Dr Watson: Sherlock Holmes' friend

3 **a** F **b** T **c** T **d** F **e** T **f** T **g** F **h** T

4 **a** in the Hotel Cosmopolitan **b** 21st December **c** James Ryder, the under-manager of the hotel

5 Blue Carbuncle stolen: 21st December
Henry Baker attacked: 24th December
Peterson got goose: 24th December
Blue Carbuncle found: 27th December

7

b	
Up to 22nd December	Mrs Oakshott
22nd-23rd December	Mr Breckinridge
23rd-24th December	Mr Windigate
24th December	Mr Henry Baker

Tapescripts

LESSON 1
Describing Your Room

Activity 2b

CORINNE There's a lot of red in my room. It's my favourite colour and I like it here because it makes the room very warm. I've got a red futon, and red spot lights, a red blind which makes the room very cosy. I've also got red supports for my book shelves so it takes up the same colour scheme again, um...

INTERVIEWER ... and there's the cushion on the box just down there.

CORINNE This is a cushion from Greece which I got many years ago, bought in central Greece and again it's the same red and it echoes my rug which is I think a central thing in the room.

INTERVIEWER Yes, that's really beautiful. Would you like just to talk about the patterns and colours?

CORINNE The patterns are diagonals, zig-zags like in the cushion cover. Now the colours remind me of Crete and that's particularly why I bought it. There are brick reds, there are dark maroons and a couple of shades of blue which remind me of the colours you see in Cretan sky and sea. Very intense colours.

INTERVIEWER Beautiful. Now there's a lot of wood in this room as well. Some very interesting boxes under the windows.

CORINNE I found these boxes and they're extremely useful. They didn't look very good when I got them and I cleaned them up myself.

INTERVIEWER The desk in the corner, it isn't a desk at all, is it? What do you use it for?

CORINNE It looks just like a desk but it is in fact my music cupboard. It has a cassette player inside and all the cassettes. It's the only place I can hide such things in this very small room.

INTERVIEWER And the table. It's a very strange shape.

CORINNE It's an octagonal table. It's a folding table which suits the small room, but I chose it to be octagonal because I've got octagonal plates.

LESSON 2
Talking about Your Favourite Day

Activity 3

ANNA My favourite day is Saturday, mainly because it's different from the rest of the week. In the week I go to school, but on Saturdays I'm a receptionist in a hotel.

I get up at 7 o'clock and then I go to work for 8 o'clock. After the guests check out, the hotel is quiet so then I can write my essays. At lunch time, which is 1 o'clock, I get my money and I have an hour's lunch break, so then I go to the shop and buy things for the evening - tights and hair spray - and I go home to lunch. About 2 o'clock I go back to the hotel and after my lunch I'm usually quite sleepy, so I fall asleep for an hour. I

only fall asleep lightly so I can wake up when someone comes into reception, and then I do some more work - essays, and then people start arriving for the evening so I check them in. About 5 o'clock I finish at the hotel so I go home. I eat my dinner and I have a shower and get ready to go out for the evening. This is my highlight of the day. This is what it's all been building up to.

I get the bus to town and I meet some friends about 9 o'clock. We usually go to watch a band. I don't get home until really late because Saturday is my only evening out when I can really enjoy myself without having to worry about getting up in the morning the next day.

LESSON 5
Ideas For Vocabulary

Activity 2

PROFESSOR BLACK There is no one way which is the best way to learn. Everyone is different. Some people learn best lying on the floor, listening to pop music. Other people like to work at a desk in a quiet room. The important thing is to find out what is best for you.

There are some useful techniques. If you find your work boring, then stop because you will learn nothing.

Also, the brain gets tired quite quickly. For example, if you work for two hours you will find that at the beginning you are fresh or ready for work. You can think clearly. After 30 or 40 minutes you begin to feel tired and you cannot think clearly. After 1 1/2 hours it gets better. Your brain knows you will stop soon. What does this tell us? You have worked too long - for one hour your brain has been tired. You need to divide your time into 30 minutes of study and have a five minute break, then you can study for another 30 minutes and take another break. This way you will think clearly for two hours. If you think clearly, you will remember better.

Exercise also helps by increasing the blood in the brain. Also it is very important to relax - listen to music or go outside. Now, you will know there are two types of memory. Long term memory and short- term memory. Long-term memory helps you remember for a long time. Short-term memory is for a short time: for example, you remember a telephone number when you dial the number. When you are learning a language the new words will go into the short-term memory first. If you want to remember these words, you have to help them to go into the long-term memory. There are many ways to do this. I will talk about two.

First you have to understand the word. If you don't understand you cannot remember. There are different ways to do this. You can make a picture in your mind. If *table* is a new word, then you see a room with a table in it. Then you might try to see the word *table* in your mind. Or you can listen to the sound and compare it with a word in your language. All the time you must make a link, that is, join the new word with something you know. Another point. It is not good to learn words on their own. For example, if you try and learn the names of objects in the house such as *washing machine, tin opener, armchair, toothbrush* you will find it difficult because these objects come from different rooms in a house. It's easier to group new words. For example, in the sitting room you find *armchairs, small tables, a TV, a sofa*. This helps your brain make a picture and helps it to organise the words for the long-term memory.

One final, but very important, technique to help you remember is to revise. You need to look at your words again and again and again. For example, on day one you start to learn a new word. On day two you look at it again for a minute or two; on day three look again maybe for a minute. The more you do this, the better you remember. You remember best with a little every day.

UNIT 3 AUCTION

LESSON 8
Describing Objects

Activity 2

AUCTIONEER Good afternoon ladies and gentlemen, and welcome to this afternoon's auction. We start with a group of items belonging to Colonel George brought by his family from all over the world. Item number 1 is a Turkish knife, first world war vintage. Brought back in 1917. This knife has a curved blade and a very unusual handle. I'd like to open the bidding, if I may please, at £20. Can I hear £20? £20, thank you very much sir. Any advance on 20?

Can I hear 22? 22 thank you. Any advance on that? 22, 25, thank you very much sir. £25 from the gentleman with the moustache at the back. 25 any advance on 25, 25. 26, 27, thank you sir, 27, 27, 28, yes thank you. Any advance on 28? £30, £30. Can I hear more? £30 going, going, £30 sold to the gentleman with the moustache. Thank you very much sir.

Item number 2 is a fine plate, round, blue representing two birds, two cocks on it. This plate is Greek. Can I hear an opening bid please? £5, thank you very much. £5 any advance on 5? Can I hear 6? £6, thank you very much, £6 any advance on that? Any advance on that? £8, thank you very much madam. £8, £8 can I hear more? Can I hear more? £10. £10. Any advance on £10 for this fine blue plate? £10 once, twice, sold. Thank you madam.

Now item number 3 is an African piece, a wooden antelope 6 inches tall, probably about 50 years old. I would like to open the bidding there if I may at £3. £3, thank you sir, £3, 4, £4, thank you, madam, yes, thank you very much. Any advance on 6, £8. Thank you £8 any more, any more? Can we take it up to 10? £10, can I hear? Yes, thank you very much sir, yes £10 for the antelope. Any more, £10. Any more? £10 going once, twice. The wooden antelope is sold to the gentleman at the side. Thank you sir.

Item number 4 is a map. It's a map of an island in the South Pacific. Bought originally as a treasure map but the clues unfortunately have gone astray. The date on the map is 1897. I would like to open the bidding if I may at £20. Can I hear £20? £20 this is, this could be a good buy, it is a treasure map. £20. No? OK no, then the item is withdrawn.

UNIT 4 A WEEKEND AWAY

LESSON 11
Choosing Leisure Activities

Activity 3

INTERVIEWER Nicky, I believe you're going to the Sherwood Forest Holiday village for your holiday this year. Why did you choose it?

NICKY Well, a number of reasons really. Firstly ... a lot of people have recommended it quite highly saying there are a lot of things to do for small children and as Joanna is now eighteen months old we thought it would be a useful place for us to go and where Jeff and I could enjoy ourselves and there'd be plenty to do for a young child.

INTERVIEWER And what are you looking forward to most of all?

NICKY Well, I don't know. There seem to be so many different things you can do there. It covers lots of activities which can take place indoors, so it doesn't matter about the weather. I suppose the wonderful swimming pool looks the most exciting thing, but there are lots of other things to do for adults such as tennis, you can hire bicycles, and do a number of activities doing things like jacuzzis which I haven't tried before. No, I'm looking forward to a whole range of activities really.

UNIT 5 EXHIBITION

LESSON 13
Describing People

Activity 4c

PAM Well I recognise him, don't you?

JUDITH No who is it?

PAM That's JR.

JUDITH No, I never saw the television programme.

PAM Yes, he's got on his smart suit.

JUDITH I don't think his hat goes with his suit. That sort of cowboy hat.

PAM Very smart suit and tie and belt.

JUDITH Um, he looks a bit of a menacing character though, doesn't he?

PAM Yes, a bit frightening, and who's the old man sitting on the chair?

JUDITH ... that's Picasso, isn't it?

PAM Oh is it? I didn't know he looked like that.

JUDITH Is he still alive?

PAM Don't think so.

JUDITH He looks pretty fit there. Big mouth he's got, hasn't he, and quite keen eyes.

PAM Bald, but not quite bald.

JUDITH Bit left round the ears. I like his trousers. My father wears trousers like that with a big check.

JUDITH Oh, look at the old woman. Looks very respectable.

PAM Doesn't she? Doesn't she look sweet? Who is it?

JUDITH That's Agatha Christie, isn't it? Wrote the crime novels.

PAM Really?

JUDITH Think so.

PAM I didn't know she looked like that.

JUDITH No, neither did I. I think I can just see it written behind her, behind her rather large legs. She looks as if she's had some problems with those legs.

PAM Looks sweet, looking through those glasses.

JUDITH Nice little dress like my grandmother used to wear.

PAM And that pearl necklace.

JUDITH   And who's she? She looks like my daughter.

PAM   I don't think that's a she. I think it's a he.

JUDITH   What?!

PAM   Yes. I think it's a pop star, um ...

JUDITH   Oh, Boy George.

PAM   That's the one.

JUDITH   Yes the one that got into trouble over drugs.

PAM   Yes, he did, didn't he, yes. That long hair, braided.

JUDITH   He makes quite a pretty girl.

PAM   Wearing lots of makeup. And that hat. He always wore that hat, didn't he? And the hair in plaits.

JUDITH   And great big shoes, or boots or something all laced up.

PAM   And lipstick and nail varnish.

UNIT 6 FESTIVALS

LESSON 16
Hallowe'en

Activity 5

JOHN The whole of our street in Cambridge celebrates an American Hallowe'en.

INTERVIEWER And what does that involve?

JOHN Ah, well you have to buy a pumpkin, a great round football-shaped vegetable and they spend a long time cutting the lid off it, scooping out the inside, removing all of the pulp, which is inside. And then they cut holes in the pumpkin, two eyes, a funny nose and a big mouth with a grin. And then they put a candle inside the pumpkin ... and they put the lid on it and place that in the window ...

Activity 7

... then they all get lots of face paints, sort of like makeup you put on your face and put horrible faces on. And when it gets towards evening, they dress up with sort of curtains or shawls or things all around them and they go out up and down the street saying, um... and they (sound of knock) knock on the door and when you open it, you see this little crowd of children all standing there and they say 'Trick or Treat?, Trick or Treat?' and that means 'give us something, or else we'll play a trick on you'. Now, I don't know what the tricks are that they play, I mean, I've heard that you get water thrown over you or they squirt you or something.

INTERVIEWER Oh dear.

JOHN ...but, um, for the treat they have a sort of bag with them and you're meant to put something in it for them.

INTERVIEWER Sweets or something like that?

JOHN Well yes, we try not to give them sweets we sort of give them apples if we've had a lot of apples that autumn so... they run around until very late sort of pretending to be ghosts, jumping out and frightening people, that kind of thing.

LESSON 17
Ghost Stories

Activity 2

FAY MERRYWEATHER I had this really strange experience in a plane some time ago. It was in 1973, in the Autumn. I was flying from New York to Florida in, er, an American Tri-Star Flight 318. Um, we had just taken off and I went to the kitchen galley to start preparing the meals for the 180 passengers on board. Now, in the galley there's an oven for heating the meals. It has a glass door and I went to open it when suddenly I saw this face, it was a man's face in the door of the oven. It was ..., I thought I was dreaming, incredible. I shut my eyes, thinking it would go away, and when Iopened them again there was nothing to see in the glass door, so I went to open it again, and as I put out my hand the face appeared again. The same face. He looked worried and was trying to talk to me. This time I was really nervous and frightened and I decided to get some help. So I took a deep breath to feel calm and walked slowly to the flight deck to get some help.

When I got to the flight deck I spoke to John, the flight engineer and said 'Come quickly, I've got a problem.', and he got up and came back to the galley with me. When we were there, I said 'Look there's a problem. I think we've got a ghost. I can see a face in the oven door.' And John looked in the oven and there was the face. But John knew this face. It was one of his friends, Don Repo, also a flight engineer, who had died in a plane crash in Florida the year before, in 1972. As we were standing there, we both heard this voice which said 'Fire, fire in the engine.' John immediately went back and checked the engines, but there was nothing wrong. So that was the end of that, and I didn't fly on that plane again.

However, about a year later, there was a fire in one of the engines of Flight 318. The pilot landed it safely and no one was killed, but it could have been a nasty accident.

LESSON 18
Traditional Recipes

Activity 3

This is Call-A-Recipe

The recipe for today is pancakes. You need the following ingredients:

100g plain flour
1/2 teaspoon salt
1 egg
300 ml milk
and 75g butter for frying.

You also need a large mixing bowl, a whisk, a mixing spoon and a frying pan.

First of all, stir the flour and salt in a bowl. Then make a hole in the middle and add the egg and half the milk. Use the whisk and start mixing from the centre. Add the rest of the milk. Mix until the mixture is smooth. Next put a little butter in your frying pan. Heat it until it's very hot. Turn the pan to make sure the butter goes all over it. Then put two tablespoons of the mixture into the hot pan. Turn the pan to make sure the mixture goes all over it. Cook over a high heat, until the pancake is brown underneath.

Then toss it and cook the other side. Roll the pancake. Put it in the oven to keep warm and make the next one. If your first one is not very good, it's because your pan is not hot enough. Better luck with the second one!

UNIT 8 TOURIST INFORMATION

LESSON 23
Describing Holidays

Activity 1

INTERVIEWER Ian, when you visited North Wales was there anything special that you did?

IAN Um, yeah, I did one thing that I really enjoyed, I visited this place called Portmeirion which I've always wanted to go to, ... and that was really great.

INTERVIEWER Can you tell me about it?

IAN It's a really strange Welsh village built on the coast, and if you look at it you think you're in the Mediterranean, all the houses are small and they're just like little villas, they're all painted white and pink and pale blue and it's just like the most amazing thing.

INTERVIEWER And what did you do?

IAN Well, there's a hotel which is absolutely incredible as well to look at, but it's far too expensive, so I didn't stay there. I just walked around the village and had a look at it, and there's a very famous pottery there called the Portmeirion pottery.

INTERVIEWER Do you think I should go?

IAN Oh definitely, and take lots of money with you.

INTERVIEWER Joyce, can you tell me about going up Snowdon?

JOYCE Well, I went on the train because I rather thought I was too old to walk up. The coaches on the train were wooden and very ancient and very old and very very hard to sit on.

INTERVIEWER Did you enjoy the views?

JOYCE The views were all right when we started, for the sun was still shining and it was still bright, but as we went higher it got misty and wet and the views disappeared.

INTERVIEWER So you saw nothing?

JOYCE We saw, um we saw what was very near us on the track, immediately below the windows, but not .... we had no distant view at all.

INTERVIEWER Would you do it again?

JOYCE I wouldn't go on the train again, next time I would walk.

INTERVIEWER Yes... Peter, have you been to North Wales?

PETE Yes I have actually, I've been to Snowdonia once, which is a mountainous area. I went climbing in the mountains.

INTERVIEWER Did you enjoy it?

PETE Yes, it was great except it was a little bit cold, it was in the winter so I didn't get all the way up the top of Snowdon because it was very icy, so I turned back, but apart from that it was great.

Activity 3

PETE What do we need to take then to the Lakes? Obviously boots.

TIM Yeah.

PETE Socks, heavy socks. You know what it's like in the

Lakes, waterproofs.

TIM Must take waterproofs.

PETE Woolly hat, gloves. I always take a spare pair of gloves actually, get a wet day and they get very wet. Ah, what else?

TIM Compass, map ...

PETE Flash light ...

TIM Water bottle ...

PETE Er, yeah, water bottle each and a day sack each, carrying all that stuff. Are you going to take care of the food or shall I?

TIM I'll take care of the food.

PETE OK, stuff for sandwiches, cheese, biscuits...

TIM Cold meat ...

PETE Cold meat er ...

TIM Chocolate ...

PETE Yeah, chocolate, mints, something to chew, chewing gum. Er, that's about it.

TIM Yeah, that's about it.

UNIT 9 RADIO STATION

LESSON 25
Listening to a Radio Broadcast

Activity 4b

RADIO ANNOUNCER We have an exciting and amusing morning for you today. After the nine o'clock news there will be a number of surprises when the comedy star Dame Edna Everage talks about her life in Australia and chooses her records in "Desert Island Discs". Count Dracula rises from the dead at 9.45 and laughter follows in the Woody Allen Reader. At 11.00 we continue with the series on the Secret Service in "My Country Right or Wrong". Then it's back to horror at 11.47 when we hear how monsters are made for horror films. This is "Horrors" at 11.47. Now here is the weather forecast until dawn tomorrow.

Activity 5

INTERVIEWER Can you tell me exactly what you do?

MIKE I'm a sports teacher at a language school. I teach many kinds of sports including football, soccer, basket-ball, badminton and tennis. My day usually starts at about 3.30 in the afternoon and I work until 9.30 in the evening. However, I do get a break between 6 and 7 p.m. for my dinner. But it's not very long to digest the food and it's back to work again until 9.30.

INTERVIEWER What kind of music do you like to listen to?

MIKE I like the Blues very much and the song I've chosen is *Mama told me Blues*. I like the words.

Activity 6

Mama Told Me Blues

1 My mama told me, you'd better be good.
  She told me she thought that I would.
  But she didn't know
  That I never could.

2 When I was sixteen I travelled away.
  I hit the city - I thought that I'd stay.
  But I robbed Jackson's Food Store,
  I couldn't pay.

3 The police grabbed me before I could run.
  They started shooting when they saw my gun.
  Oh I just didn't know
  That crime was no fun.

4 I'm stuck in prison, some day I'll be free.
  I won't go back to that city
  'Cause I know I'll remember
  What mama told me.

LESSON 26
Listening to a Science Fiction Story

Activity 3a

NEWS READER The statue of the Siren Goddess is about eight inches high and it is made of sandstone. It is very old and very famous. It was kept in the Museum of Meridian City. It was the most valuable thing in the whole Museum. The tourists on Mars buy copies of it to take back to Earth.

Activity 3b

NARRATOR 'I'll tell you the story,' said the Inspector. 'Of course, someone was paying the thief. He was doing it for someone - probably for an important art dealer. Danny Weaver (that was the thief's name) was staying in a hotel in Meridian West. He knew that the Museum was closed on Sundays. On Saturday he walked across the city to Meridian East and went to the Museum. He looked around the Museum. The statue of the Siren Goddess was in the middle of a large room. Danny Weaver hid in a small room and waited until the Museum closed. The bell rang and the visitors left the Museum. But Danny Weaver stayed hidden. At midnight he started work.'

'But what about the guards?' I asked. 'Didn't they find Danny?'

The Inspector laughed. 'They don't have guards on Mars.' he said. 'There's usually no need for them. The officials search your bags when you leave the city. You can't leave with stolen goods.'

That was true. Now I knew why there was no crime on Mars.

'At midnight,' the Inspector went on, 'Danny got out his set of tools. The statue was in a special glass and metal box. He cut all round it very carefully. His plan was very simple. He had a copy of the statue with him. He was going to take out the real statue and put the copy in the box in its place. Then he was going to go back and hide in the small room. On Monday morning, he was going to join the crowds of visitors to the Museum and go out with them.

'Then he got a terrible shock. It was 8.30 in the morning and he was not expecting anyone. He knew the Museum was closed on Sundays. But there were noises - Danny dropped his tools and the statue and ran. Out in the street, he got another shock. People were on their way to work. Everyone was busy. What had gone wrong?

'The police found him easily. Only visitors from the Earth made that mistake. We have an international dateline on Earth, but it's in the Pacific Ocean. They have a dateline on Mars, too, but it goes through a city - Meridian City. In Meridian West it was Sunday - but in Meridian East it was only Saturday. Danny hadn't thought of that problem.

We all felt sorry for Danny.

Then I asked, 'What happened to Danny?'

'There are no prisons on Mars,' said the Inspector.

'He was given a special job to do for six years. He became a guard at the Museum in Meridian City!'

'And what about the men who were paying him?' I asked. 'Did you catch them?'

'Not yet,' said the Inspector. He turned to the art dealer, Mr Maccar. The art dealer was very quiet. 'Do you think we will catch the men Danny was working for?' he asked. The Inspector looked carefully at Mr Maccar. 'You don't look very well,' he said. 'Would you like one of my space-sickness pills, Mr Maccar?'

'No thank you,' said the art dealer. His voice was as cold as ice. It gave me a shock. I looked from him to the Inspector and back again. They both had strange looks on their faces.

'This is going to be an interesting journey,' I thought to myself, 'very interesting indeed.'